NUTRITION AND YOUR BODY

— Understanding Nature's Secret of Balance —

By
BENJAMIN COLIMORE, M.A.
and
SARAH STEWART COLIMORE, L.P.T.

Design by: GERRY KELCHNER

NUTRI TION & YOUR BODY

Benjamin Colimore, M.A.
Sarah Stewart Colimore, L.P.T.

LIGHT WAVE PRESS　　　　　LOS ANGELES

Library of Congress Catalogue Card Number:
74-76118
ISBN: 0-89031-015-7

MANUFACTURED IN THE UNITED STATES OF AMERICA

Copyright © 1974 by Light Wave Enterprises

First Printing, 1974
Second Printing, 1975
Third Printing, 1976
Revised & Updated

Light Wave Enterprises
3151 Wilshire Boulevard
Los Angeles, California 90010

Printed in U.S.A.

iv

ERRATA SHEET

(Please insert where indicated)

moisten and adhere

PAGE 174 —
These two lines complete the top paragraph.

dealing with the extension of this law on to the planet and into the universe.

PAGE 182 — Insert after No. 5).

6) Phosphorus: Since the Ca:P ratio in the blood should be 10:4, the dietary ratio should be the same, 2½:1. Otherwise, calcium may be deplenished and the blood will draw from teeth and bones to restore proper ratio.

7) Magnesium at about one half the amount of dietary calcium for the same reason.

Phosphorus, the mineral most closely associated with calcium, is the one most abundantly available in

PAGE 202 — Replaces item 14.

14. Wooster, Jr., H.A. & Blanck, F.C., *Nutritional Data*, Heinz Nutritional Research Division, Mellon Institute, Pittsburgh Pennsylvania, 1949. p 55.

PAGE 203 — Replaces items 11. through 16.

11. Kleiner, Ph.D.Israel S., *Human Biochemistry,* 2nd Edition, C.V. Mosby. St. Louis. 1948., p. 364.
12. Orton & Neuhaus, *Op. Cit.* p. 192.
13. *Ibid.*
14. Wooster, Jr., & Blanck, F.C., *Nutritional Data*, H.J. Heinz Co., Pittsburgh, 1949. p. 11.
15. *Ibid.* p. 12.
16. *Ibid.* p. 13.

This book is not intended to promote the sale of any specific food, food supplement, or vitamin product. It is intended to be promoted and sold solely as a book containing the personal opinions and recommendations of the authors. Purchasers are not authorized to display or sell the book in connection with any food or vitamin product nor to use it for the purpose of promoting any such product.

This book is intended to give people who are health minded a scientific guide to balanced, high quality nutrition. It is inspired and based largely upon the research and twenty years of dedicated professional service of Robert Craig Stewart, D.C. To his memory this book is dedicated.

In addition, the authors wish to thank Thornton I. Shaw, D.C. for his invaluable professional advice in formulating the information about the colon and matters relating thereto.

INTRODUCTION TO SECOND EDITION
by W.D. CURRIER, M.D.

NUTRITION AND YOUR BODY fills a need for the layman that I have not seen done so well before. Complicated bodily functions are explained more simply, yet accurately, than I could have imagined.

Every human body, or any other living animal or plant, is a chemical factory. When we get sick chemistry, we develop disease. Essentially all disease is man-made and results from the errors of living. The greatest error of living is the error of eating. In my opinion, this is more deleterious than all the other errors combined. Hence, fundamentally, disease need not be and can be prevented.

The patient's symptoms and complaints are indications of disease. The physician must not only listen to what the patient tells him, but he must also *believe* them. Laboratory findings are usually only a minor link in the chain to the diagnosis, and the physical examination supplies only about 7% of the vital facts of a diagnostic workup.

In medical school, I remember many times the ill patient had seen so many doctors and had such a huge medical record that the professors would figuratively point their finger at such a patient and infer that they were "doctor shopping" or that they were a hypochondriac. This happened so many times with the patient that finally they felt guilty for being sick and would become fearful of relating all of their symptoms and complaints when actually it was the doctor who was at fault. He subconsciously felt guilty himself for not knowing what to do for this patient, and so, all too frequently, he overreacted. It takes so much humility, compassion, and understanding gained through years of practice for the young doctor to grow into the physician that we love and respect.

—W.D. CURRIER, M.D.

FOREWORD

I have known Sarah and Benjamin Colimore for many years. They both are living examples of what good nutrition can do for one's life. Mrs. Colimore has operated and managed one of the finest health food restaurants in Los Angeles for many many years. This business has certainly given her not only a good theoretical background for proper nutrition but has also given her practical experience in the actual preparation of many of the foods which are written about in this book.

I found this book to be easy to understand for the lay reader and one which will give practical basic information in a pleasant style. This is especially important in an age when many of the books written about nutrition are complex and frequently "lose the reader"due to the use of too much technical jargon. Once the reader completes this book, he or she will have a firm knowledge that will be most useful in understanding nutritional matters. The analogies used are excellent and carefully thought out by the authors. Although the statement has been made that "you are what you eat", this is not exactly a true statement. The balance of a proper life formula must consist of adequate exercise as well as a proper psychological approach to stress situations. A well balanced life which measures nutrition, exercise and mental attitude is one that no doubt will add years to anyone's life and will not only add years to life but will add life to years.

I again congratulate the authors on what is a fine

endeavor and which will be a most important addition to the field of books written on the most interesting subject of nutrition.

Ronald M. Lawrence, M.S., M.D.

March 24, 1974   Ronald M. Lawrence, M.S. M.D.

Laurel Canyon Medical Clinic
North Hollywood, California

TABLE OF CONTENTS

ix

blueprint for our physical life, protected in the nucleus of each cell.

Organ	Tissue Maintenance:	Fat Metabolism:	Carbohydrate Metabolism:
Brain	Inositol, B1		B1, B2, B3, Pantothenic Acid
Heart	B1, B6		
Liver	B3, B6, Choline Biotin	B6, Pantothenic Acid, Choline, Inositol	
Kidneys	Choline		
Gastrointestinal	B1, B3, Pantothenic Acid		
Muscles	Pantothenic Acid, B1, Choline, Biotin	Pantothenic Acid B6	B1, B2, B3, Pantothenic Acid, Inositol
Nerves	B1, B3, Biotin	B6, Pantothenic Acid	B1, B2, B3, Pantothenic Acid Inositol
Blood	B3, B6, Choline, B12, Folic Acid	Inositol, Choline	
Eye	B2		
Epidermis	B6		

Nutritional Co-enzyme placement of Various B Complex Vitamins with Tissue, Body Fats, and Energy production from Carbohydrate.

TABLE OF CHARTS & DIAGRAMS

xiii

The Doctor of the future will give no medicine, but will interest his patients in the care of the human frame, in diet, and in the cause and prevention of disease.

—Thomas A. Edison

No physician worthy of the name, . . .can take the position that ignorance about nutrition is preferable to understanding.

. . .A multidisciplinary approach involving not only biochemistry and physiology, but also internal medicine, pathology, microbiology, dentistry, endocrinology, reproduction, and other related areas, is urgently needed.

—Dr. Roger J. Williams from his minority report to President Nixon, as a member of the President's Advisory Panel on Heart Disease, 1972.

VITAMIN-MINERAL:	TISSUE REPAIR & MAINTENANCE	FATTY ACID METABOLISM	CARBOHYDRATE METABOLISM
A	Epithelial health, liver storage.	Reduce acetone buildup.	
B	SEE SEPARATE CHART p.xii		
C	Collagen, adrenals, phagocytes, cell respiration.		
D	Activates amino acid carriers for calcium.	Reduces acetic acid buildup.	
E	Removal of scar tissue.	Prevents peroxidation.	
K	Manufacture of fibrin for blood clotting.	Reduces alcohol buildup.	
CALCIUM	Bones, muscles, nerves, heart.	Immoderate fat intake interferes with calcium.	
MAGNESIUM	Muscles, nerves, heart.		Activates B1
PHOSPHORUS	Bones, muscles, nerves, brain, red cells.	Forms high energy bonds in fat and carbohydrate metabolism.	
SODIUM	Adrenals, tissue fluid balance, plasma buffer, kidneys.		
POTASSIUM	Tissue fluid balance, heart, kidneys, nerves.		
ZINC	Insulin synthesis in pancreas, prostate, bones.		
IRON	Oxygen carrier in hemoglobin.		
IODINE	Thyroid.		
COPPER	Forms red cells, hemoglobin, cell respiration.		
MANGANESE		Prevents fatty liver	Enzymes for forms, glucose metabolism.

Nutritional placement of Vitamin and Mineral Co-enzymes with Tissue, Body Fats and Energy Production from Carbohydrate.

AN INTRODUCTION BY THE AUTHORS

What we have tried to do above all else in the following pages is to stress the importance of consuming a balance of nutrients at each meal and to demonstrate what we mean by organizing practical food plans for each meal of the day. As we proceed, we have reinforced the necessity of nutritional balance and careful food planning with biochemical and physiological explanations of man's digestive and metabolic systems.

From our encounters with literally hundreds of people every day, we have observed that few people think and therefore eat in terms of balanced nutrition. From casual conversations, from questions asked in our classes and lectures, and from consultations held in our office, we find that people choose individual foods based on whether or not the food is

xvii

fattening, how tasty it is, or whether it is a "pure" food. They think, more often, no further than the meal in front of them and thereby fail to consider the total balanced nutritional intake for the entire day. After they gain a fundamental understanding of how to balance their essential nutrients at each meal, however, many complaints such as hunger between meals, unwanted pounds, poor elimination, and exhaustion at the end of the day disappear.

Today, more so than ever before, there is a wealth of nutritional information available. Some authors, highly qualified in their fields, have written comprehensive and enthusiastic treatises covering virtually every area of nutrition. Others, giving us the benefit of specialized research, have concentrated on one or two areas in the field of nutrition. Still other writers, espousing specific life styles, have taken nutritional approaches that support various philosophical or metaphysical systems. Each of these approaches has its own value, but the flood of information — and sometimes misinformation — makes it difficult for many people to organize the salient features in their minds, and so frequently their knowledge remains fragmentized. Consequently, many who are pursuing healthful living have, for one reason or another, ultimately overlooked the necessity of the critical nutritional balance that produces efficient digestion, metabolism, and elimination. We have found that many people who are serious about healthful living have been distracted and have fixated their attention on the amazing function and the overriding yet ultimately transitory importance of just one or two of the many contributing factors to good nutrition.

The preamble to our book then is simply this: *Our health is not contingent on any one factor — not protein, not Vitamin E, not herbs, no, not even Vitamin C or chelated minerals, for there is no miracle food or food supplement that will do the entire job. There is only the high quality, sufficient quantity, and proper balance of all nutrients and the efficiency of their enzyme systems. They are all important.* They all have their proper place, and as we see it, the need now in the field of nutrition is to define clearly each of these places. The need then is really for *perspective* — to select, reorganize, and bring into clearer scientific focus the important elements of that vast body of information which has accumulated in the field of nutrition; organize it, that is, in terms of daily eating: first, in the light of our body's chemistry, and secondly, in plans by which we combine our foods at those three meals we eat daily to maintain a healthy chemistry.

There is no shortcut. For proper efficiency, Nature demands the balance of high quality nutrition, and this is what we want to give our readers through the information and practical applications we set forth. *Balance is Nature's incontrovertable law,* and in illuminating the conditions she sets down for us, we hope to serve both Nature and Science and provide a guide for the layman, a primer, so to speak, of the fundamentals of nutritional science through an understanding of the balance of nutritional quality and quantity which with Nature we use to build, maintain and energize efficient human bodies.

—THE AUTHORS

CHAPTER ONE:

AN OVERVIEW

Nature, the transformation of energy from one form to another, universally expresses itself in three specific patterns. The first of such patterns swirls in *rotary* motion, evident in the movement of the atom, the human cell, the planets, our entire solar system, and all ordered movements of swirling spheres, evolving on the cosmic scale as a grand replica of the parent atom. The second of such patterns moves in *spirals*, evident in the mysterious helix of the chromosomes which stores the genetic blueprint for *each* cell in *each* cellular nucleus of the human body, evident in whirlpools swirling in great bodies of water, in the violent cone of a tornado sweeping across a midwestern plain, or in the fiery vortex that rises from a missile site at the moment of launching. Still a third pattern of energy thrusts itself *forward* to initiate some dramatic, evolutionary step in the universe: the passionate emission of sperm, the delicate growth of an embryo's spine, the rapid transportation of blood through the vascular system, or the overwhelming bolt of an electric current through an illumined skyscraper.

To give these patterns their free range of expression, nature takes the energy assembled in one form, disassembles it into the particles that supplied the form's energy, and reassembles them into a new form. When the new form follows closely upon the old, we readily recognize the transitory nature of the disassembling period. But when in some cases we cannot perceive any emerging new form, we specify the disassembling period as death. Death, for most investigators, declares an end to the old form — Period! But as a footnote, it reflects proportionately our scientific incapacity to measure that further movement of the energy released from the old form.

Yet out of the myriad changes of energy patterns that *are* measurable in the universe, there is one grouping of transformations to which many of us lately are giving more thought and attention. In fact, people have currently become interested in their bodies as fields of energy transformations, discovering how to observe more intelligently the conditions that nature has imposed upon us for building and maintaining that constant flow of energy exchange within us.

In our bodies, the movements of energy which we spoke of— rotary, spiral, and forward— present the evidence of Nature at work disassembling the particles of one life form and reassembling them into another. The laws governing this transformation constitute the science of nutrition, a science that begins with food, a life form without, which becomes the cell, the life form within. Let us begin then with those foods most suitable for Nature's work of transformation:

EGGS MILK FISH CHEESE MEAT NUTS FRUIT
                                FOWL SEEDS
                                        GRAINS
                                        VEGETABLES
                                        LEGUMES

Among these foods, nature distributes three forms of energy called PROTEIN, FAT, and CARBO-HYDRATE, the *essential nutrients*. Some of the staple foods contain all of the essential nutrients, others contain two, while still others contain only one in any significant quantity. How they overlap may be clarified in the following diagram:

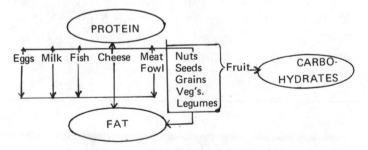

Nature's transformation of food into cells begins with the first stage of nutrient release, *ingestion*. Ingestion consists simply of thoroughly masticating and swallowing the food in order to trigger the second stage of release, *digestion*.

Digestion is the process whereby our body starts actually to transform the food energy by breaking down the protein, fat, and carbohydrate into micro-nutrient particles that become the building blocks of our body's mass and energy. The digestive processes reduce the protein foods to their *amino acids* and *nucleic acids*. They reduce the fat to *fatty acids*, and the carbohydrates to *glucose* or blood sugar. The forms of amino and nucleic acids, fatty acids, and glucose are simple enough to be carried through the body's elaborate transport system to the cell, thus another corollary arises from the laws of transformation: ONLY THE SIMPLEST OF MATERIALS MAY ENTER THE BLOODSTREAM AND PASS INTO THAT SPHERE OF FLUID ENERGY, THE CELL.

— THE EGG IS I —

To feed the cell, to maintain its life and well-being, is the only reason we eat. To better understand the cell as a unit of life, we can compare it to one of its larger, more familiar analogues, the egg. The egg, we know, consists of a circular yolk engulfed in a clear

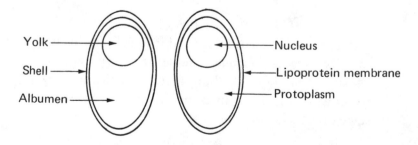

FIG. 1:   Comparison of the Components of an Egg with the Components of the Human Cell.

liquid called albumen. Both the yolk and the albumen are encased by a brittle wall called the shell. Each cell in the human body is broadly similar to the parts of the egg. The yolk is the cell's nucleus; the albumen is the protoplasm; and the "shell" holding it all together is the lipoprotein membrane, or simply, the cell wall.

So much for the general similarities. Let's now look at some of the cell's specific differences. Our cell wall, of course, is not a brittle calcium composition like the egg shell. Imagine, rather, a network of interlacing strands, much like a seamless nylon stocking, but not quite. Instead of nylon, the netlike composition is a mixture of fat (lipid) and protein. Only through the pores of this lipoprotein membrane can the cell obtain its nutrition. The cell wall must therefore be kept permeable so that the amino and nucleic acids, the fatty acids, and the glucose (a bead of liquid sugar) can pass through. How these micro-nutrients are driven in their forward movement through the body's elaborate transport system to accomplish their osmotic passage into the rotating energy of the cell, and how the cell continues the transformation is called *metabolism*.[1] Metabolism, the creation of mass and energy out of the simplest micronutrients, is what our physical preconscious life is all about.

Picture now, at the threshold of the cell wall, the arrival of the amino and nucleic acids from food protein, the fatty acids from food fat, and the glucose from food carbohydrate. The first task of these nutrients is to nourish the cell wall. This is the job of certain amino and fatty acids. They combine and form a new mass called lipoprotein. As lipoprotein they repair and strengthen, or if necessary, completely rebuild a cell wall.[2] Next, the remainder of the fatty acids and the glucose pass osmotically through the pores of the cell wall to be oxidized, i.e., burned up, in the protoplasm for energy. This naturally requires oxygen which enters the cell in the same manner as the other nutrients, through the porous lipoprotein wall. This passage of oxygen is called *respiration*.

But how does the cell dispose of the waste produced by its oxidations? There appears in the protoplasm a group of inverted bubbles called vacuoles.[3] Into these vacuoles, the cell deposits the waste materials resulting from the oxidation of glucose and fatty acids. Since the cell is in continual movement due to the property of latent heat characterizing the rotary movement of spheroid forms, the desultory movement of the vacuoles eventually brings them to the edge of the cell wall, and they pass through its pores into the bloodstream. This ejection of waste material is called *excretion*.

No cell can maintain its metabolic cycle of metabolism, respiration, oxidation, and excretion indefinitely. The cell must "die" so that other transformations of energy may continue on the broader, more inclusive planetary scale. The life cycle of a healthy cell is normally 120 days. After 120 days, the old cell decomposes and a duplicate cell takes its place. Its precise structure is due to the blueprint stored in the preceding nucleus and transmitted to the new nucleus so exact duplication can occur. Each nucleus, then, must be nourished with nucleic acid from food protein in order to sustain, by means of a genetic code, the plan for the structure of the entire body. The genetic code is an arrangement of permanent atoms transferred from cell lifetime to cell lifetime to maintain the unity and integrity of each cell. This is the process of cell *reproduction*.

— SUMMING IT UP —

And so we have the complete cycle of transformation: First, *ingestion*, whereby food nutrients, protein, fats, and carbohydrates are masticated and swallowed. Second, *digestion*, whereby these nutrients are broken down into amino and nucleic acids, fatty acids, and glucose. Third, *metabolism*, whereby the process of all cell nutrition begins with certain amino and fatty acids combining to make the cell wall. Fourth, *respiration*, the continuation of metabolism, whereby oxygen is brought into the cell so that fatty acids and glucose may undergo oxidation to make heat and energy. Fifth, *excretion*, the conclusion of metabolism, whereby the waste products of oxidation are dumped into vacuoles and floated out of the cell. Sixth, *reproduction*, whereby the nucleic acids which entered the nucleus in the metabolic cycle transmit the genetic blueprint from one cellular lifetime to another.[4] This cycle and its many aspects serve as the foundation for each of the succeeding chapters. Our object is to uncover and explore the most important pathways of energy provided by the body. What we want to discover is how to keep these pathways open and clear, and how to combine high quality nutrients to insure their efficiency. In this regard, the first lesson we must learn is *balance*.

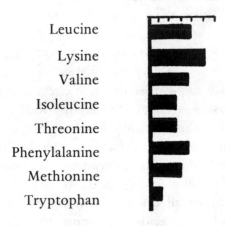

Leucine
Lysine
Valine
Isoleucine
Threonine
Phenylalanine
Methionine
Tryptophan

Amino Acid ratios for maximum assimilation of protein.

CHAPTER TWO:

THE COMMON DENOMINATOR

Balance is nature's incontrovertable law. It is a fact we cannot emphasize enough. In nature, all cycles, polarities, rhythms are governed by balance. The same is true of all energy, including energy obtained from nutrients in our food. Combining foods for balance of *essential nutrients* is the fundamental basis for preparing meals. To the three essential nutrients we have already mentioned — PROTEIN, FAT, and CARBOHYDRATES — we will add two more, VITAMINS and MINERALS. Collectively, they constitute the common denominator for each meal of the day's total intake. An overabundance or the neglect of any one of them will cause problems in digestion and metabolism. A consistent overabundance of protein, for example, can eventually result in gout; whereas, an oversupply of oils and fats can congest not only the blood stream, but the liver and the lymphatics as well. Too many carbohydrates will convert to unwanted adipose tissue in those parts of the body where too many extra pounds put a strain on the body's critical organs. An oversupply of certain fat soluble vitamins will cause a temporary toxicity. Too many minerals administered unwisely will create unwanted deposits in bodily fluids, joints, and arteries. *In other words, too much of a good thing is just about as bad as not enough,* for too much will congest the metabolic pathways we want to keep clear. On the other hand, omit any of these fundamental nutrients and you cheat the cells of needed nutrition. These cells, these tissues, these organs must be served wisely and faithfully, for the energy they enrich us with is only proportionate to the energy we invest in them. If we balance each meal with the five basic nutrients, the problems arising from excesses, so unfortunately prevalent today, will no longer trouble us. In like manner, the deficiencies which invariably accompany such excesses and which many researchers have classified as symptoms of malnutrition will also disappear. In this chapter, we will define protein, demonstrate how it is digested and metabolized in the body, and how breakfast is the meal in which protein should play a major role. Our formulated breakfast menus offer detailed and balanced ways to get not only protein but all three basic nutrients to fortify in satisfying but not inflated amounts.

Whenever we eat a protein food, we are taking into our bodies the largest food molecule that exists. Each protein molecule consists of no less than seven elements:

Carbon C
Hydrogen . . . . . . .H
Oxygen . . . . .O
Sulphur . . . . .S

Iron . . . . Fe
Phosphorus . . . . P
Nitrogen . . . . N

By now most of our readers know generally the foods which contain substantial amounts of the protein molecule and are labeled "the protein foods":

EGGS, MILK, FISH, CHEESE, MEAT AND FOWL, SEEDS-NUTS-GRAINS-VEGETABLES-LEGUMES.

The order in which we have listed these protein foods is not arbitrary. Since the availability of usable protein varies from food to food, we have listed them in the order of biologically available protein. We will explain what this means.

The key to the value of the protein molecule lies in its nitrogen, the most important of its seven elements. It is the Nitrogen which yields nucleic acids and amino acids to build body protein. These acids are so critical that were we deprived of them, it would be impossible for our cells to build, maintain, and repair any body tissue. In addition, the liver would be unable to form indispensible hormones and enzymes, and the blood stream could not transport minerals. This is how nature executes the law of balance. She will take a combination of elements such as those acids constituting the energy of Nitrogen in food protein, break them all apart and reassemble them in a carefully constructed new combination such as those constituting the cells of our bodies. What is it but analysis and synthesis, terms we usually apply to mental operations, but which are also microconversions carried on in our bodies as often as fifty thousand times a second every day of our lives.

But whether these conversions ever happen in us depends on two conditions: First, it depends on how many and what combinations of amino acids we decide to take into ourselves in the form of food protein; and secondly, it depends on the efficiency of our digestion and metabolism. *Here, then, is where our responsibility begins— with knowledge and with a willingness to use that knowledge to act intelligently.*

Consider the first condition: There are, all together, twenty-four identifiable amino acids, used in the body. At least eight, perhaps ten,[1] of these twenty-four are *essential*, which means nature has set down further conditions which we must acknowledge and follow to obtain maximum nutritional results. First, the essential amino acids must be taken into the body in the form of food or food supplements. Second, all eight must be taken together at one time; and third, all eight must occur in a certain ratio to each other to constitute what is called a complete protein. It is nothing less than nature's irrepressible law of balance at work. If complete proteins are eaten at each meal, that is, if we eat foods containing the eight essential amino acids in their proper ratio, then the body is well able to manufacture the remaining fourteen. The essentials are:

phenylalanine	valine
leucine	lysine
isoleucine	threonine
methionine	tryptophane

Of the protein foods listed earlier, eggs, milk, fish, meat and poultry, and cheese fulfill the conditions for complete protein foods. Most seeds, many nuts, very few grains, and even fewer vegetables fulfill the same conditions. The descending order of these foods, then, indicates the high to low availability of their protein, due to variations in the ratio of the amino acids they contain. Eggs, for example, are at the top of the list because their essential amino acids are balanced in such a way that 95% of the protein is available for use in the body. The egg, therefore, is often used as a norm by which to evaluate the amino acid availability of other complete protein foods. Milk comes second with 83% of its protein available for body use. Fish is third with 80%; meat and poultry fourth with approximately 68%; and the nuts, seeds, grains and vegetable category with the widest margin of protein availability, 38-70%, with most of the ratios below 60%.[2] Be careful, then, for many of the foods in the last protein category are not complete insofar as they lack or are deficient in one or more of the essential aminos. Such a deficiency, of course, upsets the ratio and handicaps the availability of the protein, which is why strict vegetarians have difficulty acquiring enough protein if dairy products are not included in their diet. Although by eating large and varied quantities of vegetables it *is* possible to maintain a recommended daily allowance of protein, it does require a thorough and tedious study of the biological availability [3] of vegetable protein. In other words, if we choose to be vegetarians and do not base our nutrition on sufficient knowledge of amino and nucleic acid balance, our bodies are not likely to receive enough of these acids to reassemble them in the proportions required to make new cells. In the conversion process, nature is obliged to waste materials which she would certainly have been able to use if her first law had been observed by initially supplying balanced nutrition (cf. chart, p.8).

Since it is our opinion that we should depend for our protein on those foods which provide the highest biological availability, let's consider at some length the highest quality protein foods, that is, food which can be relied upon for the most efficient use of protein. In considering these foods we will emphasize not only the protein content, but also the total nutritional value of the food and any problem which may arise regarding the assimilation of other factors in the food.

— THE FOODS CONTAINING THE MOST BIOLOGICALLY AVAILABLE PROTEIN —

EGGS

In their most natural nutritional state, eggs are the product of hens exposed to natural fertilization by a rooster. Moreover, rather than being cooped up in rows of little boxes, the hens are allowed to wander around and scratch for worms in the ground. They are fed high protein diets supplemented with quality oils such as safflower oil. Consequently, the eggs of these hens are high in wholesome nutrition, the principle being that the healthier the cell, the higher the quality of its nutritional value for us.

— TOTAL NUTRITION OF THE EGG —

The summary of the ingredients of such fertile eggs consists virtually of a catalogue of most of our essential nutrients. The white is practically a pure proteinous solution containing the eight essential amino acids and consequently all but a fraction of the *total six grams of egg protein*. The yolk is a source of several vital minerals — calcium, fluorine, iron, magnesium, manganese, phosphorus, sodium, and sulphur. It also incorporates an impressive group of vitamins: A, B, D, F, and G. Riboflavin (B2) is abundant in the white as well as in the yolk. Once again, remember, if you are a vegetarian, you need the B12 in the egg to guard against anemia (cf. Chapter Six, p.157.)

Fifty-two to sixty-seven percent of the egg gives us the essential fatty acids we need, while fourteen percent is rich in lecithin— a substance composed of two important fat emulsifiers, choline and inositol—and pyrodoxine (B6), factors which help us to handle the five or six grams of fat present in the egg.

— THE CHOLESTEROL FACTOR —

While we are considering the egg as a totally balanced food, we should take time out to consider one of the reservations voiced most frequently about eggs. People ask us, "What about cholesterol in eggs?" So many people have cut down or perhaps have stopped eating eggs altogether because of their cholesterol content. But is this really advisable?

Consider the positive values of cholesterol. Its chief function appears to be as a carrier of fatty acids in the blood.[4] In addition, our bodies use cholesterol to form nerve tissue, to protect red blood corpuscles, and to afford greater solidity to the cells. The suprarenal glands attached to the kidneys utilize cholesterol in the manufacture of their hormones. And one of cholesterol's most commonly known functions is the formation of bile acids essential to the assimilation of fats.[5] The bile appears also to be the most common channel for the excretion of excess cholesterol. A healthy body manufactures a regular flow of bile which, as we shall see in Chapter Two, promotes the absorption of fat and fat soluble vitamins. We should also hasten to add that it is not dietary cholesterol alone that affects the level of cholesterol in the blood. The amount of cholesterol discharged in the blood often depends as much on the emotions of a person as on any other factor.

In view of cholesterol's positive functions and the variable emotional factor, it is really not the amount of cholesterol intake that does the real harm, but the disturbed equilibrium— balance, again— between the amount of cholesterol and the presence of those factors which commonly aid in emulsifying the whole range of fats and other "lipids" of which cholesterol is only a part.[6] These factors we've already mentioned: lecithin and B6.

Take a closer look at the cholesterol-lecithin balance of a single fertile egg, such as the one described earlier. In one such fertile egg we find approximately 194-200 milligrams (mgs.) of cholesterol, balanced by nearly 1700 mgs. of lecithin. In other words, the amount of lecithin in the fertilized egg is at least eight times the amount of cholesterol.[7] In fact, the Framingham Study reports: "Eggs contain much more lecithin than cholesterol, and therefore the intake of one or two eggs daily cannot harm us, if only the other food stuffs are well balanced, and the attitude toward life is harmonious."

MILK

Many of us are gratefully aware of the scientific methods which so carefully control the diet and health of a herd of cows that pasteurization can be avoided and the biochemistry of milk remain unaltered. Such controls consist of many preventative measures: daily bacteria counts, weekly anaerobic tests, monthly streptococci and brucella tests, blood tests on the cows every sixty days, and T.B. skin tests made every 180 days. Although these measures are important, it is principally the diet of the herd which produces the high grade milk. For example, a herd's staple diet might well be enriched by a ration of barley, oats, milo, hominy feed, brewers grain, mill run bran, beet pulp, orange pulp, cotton seed meal, molasses, kelp, corn fermentation solubles, dicalcium phosphate, yeast, and trace minerals enriched with Vitamins A, D, and E. Milk yielded from cows fed such a diet will contribute relatively more food value for less money than do the other foods comprising a meal designed to meet daily nutritional needs. Once again, the healthier the cell, the higher its nutritional value for the consumer.

— TOTAL NUTRITION OF MILK —

Raw milk produced under such scientifically controlled conditions retains all the nutritional elements to some extent burned up in pasteurization: all the enzymes, the Wulzen factor, the X factor, *100% of the protein (one gram per ounce)*, all the eighteen fatty acids — saturated and unsaturated— needed to metabolize protein and calcium; 100% of all vitamins— A, D, E, the B Complex, and Vitamin C; 100% of the mineral content— calcium, chlorine, magnesium, phosphorus, potassium, sodium, sulphur, and twenty-four trace minerals. Moreover, the carbohydrates naturally associated with the elements in milk are easily utilized in certified raw milk.

The word "certified" is extremely important and we introduce it last to emphasize this importance. The label, CERTIFIED RAW MILK, guarantees the safety and purity of the nutritional content of the milk, testifying that the milk is produced according to the local standards and controls of the American Association of Medical Milk Commissions. We might add that "certified" actually means that the milk is produced under the supervision and strong recommendation of the medical profession. Certified Raw Milk has for over fifty years been accepted in medical journals affiliated with the American Medical Association which reports that no disease has ever been traced to certified raw milk, yet 70% of milk-borne epidemics have been traced to pasteurized milk. [8] This is not unusual considering the bacteria count in raw certified milk is lower than that in pasteurized milk.

In spite of the merits of raw certified milk, at this writing, California is the only state in America which sells pure raw certified milk.[9]

— THE PASTEURIZATION PROBLEM —

Pasteurization, which is intended to protect the consumer against harmful bacteria, also unfortunately destroys much of milk's good nutrition. Pasteurization wipes out over 50% of the natural Vitamin C, anywhere from 38-80% of the B Complex, the entire Vitamin D content, and 90% of the enzymes including all of one enzyme, phosphatase, needed for the assimilation of calcium. When milk is pasteurized, factors such as the anti-ulcer factor, the growth promoting factor, and the X factor in tissue repair are destroyed. In addition, since heating toughens the bonds between the protein acids, pasteurization decreases the digestibility and biological efficiency of the milk protein, rendering the protein complex less available for the repair and rebuilding of tissues. Likewise, less available for metabolism are the essential unsaturated fats as well as the carbohydrates which are altered by the heat of pasteurization. This is simply to say that we desperately need more dairy farmers around the country who will preserve the nutritional value of natural milk by producing it under scientifically controlled conditions so that the consumer will obtain a superior grade of milk which does not have to undergo the necessary destruction of harmful bacteria through pasteurization.

— THE RENNIN FACTOR —

The most frequent complaint voiced by many adults about milk, whether it be certified raw or pasteurized, is, "I can't digest it." Like many of us, these people have discovered that after childhood, milk becomes less easily tolerated by our systems, which makes it difficult to drink on a regular basis. The reason for this is that the enzyme rennin which aids the digestion of milk in children's stomachs disappears at a fairly early age. Thereafter, milk becomes a drain on the stomach's hydrochloric acid and pepsin — two enzymes needed for protein digestion (explained later in this chapter). It is wise, then, to guard against the indigestion and flatulence sometimes caused by milk, by taking supplements of hydrochloric acid and pepsin in tablet form before-hand to enable the stomach to handle milk. Often, according to the same principle, the addition of a little fruit juice, such as apple or orange, helps to curdle the milk and break it down for easy digestion.

People who abandon whole milk because of digestive problems find a blessed relief in buttermilk which is so easily tolerated by the body. Buttermilk, which has the same amount of protein as whole milk, helps build in the intestines the friendly bacteria needed to absorb amino acids into the system. We will examine this process in Chapter Four.

MEAT, FISH, AND POULTRY

The value of these foods lies not only in their high quality, complete protein, but in the easy assimilation of it. An organically nourished steer, for example, assimilates nutrients from rich grass and grains which we have neither the special teeth to grind nor the twofold stomach to digest. The beef on our plates yields these nutrients in a form extremely digestible because it is so similar to our own tissue protein.

Poultry which has been fed a diet such as the one outlined under EGGS will store rich nutrients and abundant food synergists to expedite assimilation. The cells of fowls fed polyunsaturated oils will have a far better balanced fat content than those whose diets do not include such oils. This is important, because even though we are considering chiefly the protein content of these foods, we must be assured that the protein food as well as any other food be as completely balanced in other nutrients that should be present for the highest quality overall nutrition. *Otherwise, we are cheating ourselves, and to compensate, we end up eating a great many more equally poorly nutritious foods. This not only puts a strain on our system but leads to one of the biggest problems in America today, overeating.*

A good example of a food which is highly nutritious because it maintains a fine balance of protein with other nutrients is fish. Often richer in protein than many meats, fish contains our much needed polyunsaturated oils and an ample supply of minerals absorbed from the sea and its environment. Minerals and protein should always be taken together because, as we shall see, they work together in the body. Protein moves the minerals through the body, a principle that applies to the cell level, but which you can demonstrate just by lifting your arm. Your muscle, mainly protein, has carried your bone, basically mineral, upward.

There are currently many valid problems voiced concerning the eating of meat, fish, and poultry, not many of which we can hope to resolve here. Yet we should be aware of them in order to cope as best we can under the circumstances.

— THE HORMONE-CONTAMINATION PROBLEM —

The growing concern today is the contamination of meat from the use of hormones, tranquilizers, antibiotics, and pesticide residues. Hormones are injected into the steers in the form of stilbesterol, a synthetic compound with strong properties of the female hormone, estrogen. It is given to cattle to increase their fat, the same fat into which pesticide residues from the feed eventually settle. In addition to the traces of stilbesterol breakdown found currently in meat, authorities have also discovered traces of tranquilizers used prior to slaughtering, and antibiotics used after slaughter to prevent spoilage.

Poultry and fish likewise suffer from contamination, e.g., stilbesterol pellets are sometimes left under the skin of chickens, while other birds (once marked "acronized") have either been dipped in aureomycin or have been treated with an organic arsenic. Shore varieties of shell-fish—clams, oyster, etc.—become toxic from industrial wastes, while gutted whole fresh fish, unpeeled shrimp, and shucked scallops are

frequently treated with the antibiotic, chlortetracycline. It all adds up to a boost for the grocer's sales,
since he can keep his meat, poultry and fish a little
longer due to the treatment with antibiotics, but we
question whether it is wholesome to use antibiotics
which mask the corrosive effects of salmonella and
certain molds whose activity is not arrested by the
antibiotics and might well be spoiling the meat even
though it may still appear fresh. It is possible today,
by inquiring at health food stores across the country,
to find the scattered, more discerning raisers and
distributors of meat, fish, and poultry who guarantee
that their products are organically fed and free from
hormones and toxins. The men who tackle such a
responsibility are to be highly praised, for the
obstacles they must surmount are immense, indeed,
practically overwhelming.

It is increasingly more difficult to assess the purity
of the seafood we buy. Mercury, one of the most
frequently mentioned hazards contaminating our
waters, has been present in the sea long before
industry excreted it in excessive amounts. There have
been reports of tuna, for example, preserved for fifty
years, which upon being analysed was found to
contain a level of mercury fifty percent higher than
that level found most frequently in fish today. The
mercury which we ingest in fish forms methyl
mercury within us. Vitamin C in generous quantities
appears to chelate this mercury thereby increasing
our tolerance for it.[10] To escape the contaminated
seafood from local industrial waters, deep sea fish is
probably safer than most, but whether in some cases,
for example, antibiotics such as chlortetracycline are

added to freshly caught shrimp just before they are frozen on board ship is still questionable.

— A REALISTIC APPRAISAL —

It is no longer a matter of trying to find a place where any food at all can be grown or raised in a non-contaminated environment. It is only a matter of degree, as to which areas are less polluted than others. Realistically, it will take years to rid the soil and the sea of the pollutants that now saturate it. Since we are shamefully late in starting to purify our environment, no food that we presently eat is completely free from contamination, and is not likely to be for another five to ten years even under the most rigid ecological program. The best bargain we can make with ourselves, then, is an agreement not to further jeopardize our own health and the health of our children by depriving our bodies of critically needed nutrition for the reason that we now discover nutrition co-exists with nitrites and pesticides. This type of cell starvation, instead of winning the war will only hasten defeat.

We must support in every sensible way the growing ecological sciences that will eventually reverse the hazardous conditions in which we now find ourselves. Just as through sound body ecology we have found practical, temporary, ways to detoxify our bodies from the pollutants we take in with air and water, so must we— as this book will demonstrate— as sensibly as we know how, do the same with regard to food: First, we should continue to choose foods based on the high quality of the substantial nutrition *that remains unaltered in them*. Secondly, we should conscientiously balance these substantially nutritious foods at each meal to give the body the support it needs *to build on the cell level and begin the task of detoxification*. And thirdly, *to fortify our balanced substantial nutrition with those supplements which will intensify and secure the completion of the body's victory over toxins invading our cells.*

This is the basic plan, and if we understand the value of balanced, substantial nutrition, and how digestion and metabolism guarantee to use every valid food molecule to keep all our cells alive and vital, we will want to employ the most sensible and efficient methods to expedite their work. Let's start with balanced protein nutrition.

— THE LAB WITHIN —

To understand how the protein from the foods we have just discussed is converted by our bodies into something entirely different, we must understand the human laboratory which nature uses to accomplish the transformation of food into new mass and energy. This brings us to our first look at the digestive tract.

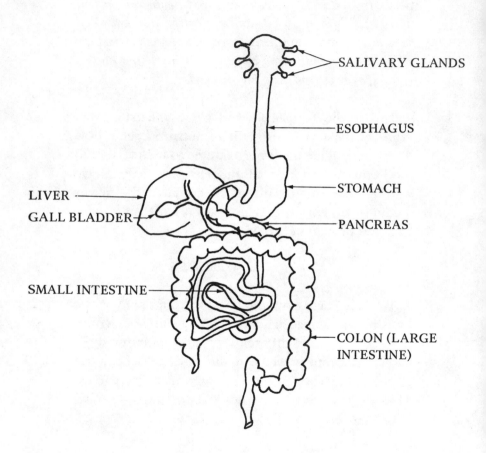

FIG. 2: Component Parts of the Human Digestive System.

— THE FIRST STAGE OF PROTEIN RELEASE —

Although all of the organs labeled in the diagram play a major part in the transformation of food energy, not all of them are involved in digesting each one of the three basic nutrients, PROTEIN, FAT, and CARBOHYDRATE. As we study the digestion of protein, we will be concerned with the four digestive organs which contribute to protein assimilation:

> The stomach
> The pancreas
> The liver
> The small intestine

— FROM CRADLE TO GRAVE —

Let's now trace the life of a protein food from the time we carry it to our mouth as a baby molecule, to the time when it enters the cell and matures, until in its old age it breaks down to disappear into the body's paths of elimination.

Whether it be in the form of dairy products, fish, meat, poultry or legumes, our first encounter finds the infant substance of the protein molecule, the amino and nucleic acids, bundled up in the Nitrogen and surrounded by the other six protective elements we mentioned earlier— Carbon (C), Hydrogen (H), Oxygen (O), Phosphorus (P), Sulfur (S), and Iron (Fe).[11] Each of these elements will follow its own metabolic pathway, once it is liberated in the body by the digestive process.[12] For the present, however, we are interested solely in the Nitrogen.

No real breakdown in the protein molecule begins until it reaches the stomach. Here we come into contact with the first group of digestive workers, the enzymes. *Enzymes are extremely small protein molecules formed by the body out of the protein we eat, which break down larger food proteins into smaller units that can eventually be used to build and maintain cells.* Some protein enzymes, called *synergists* are contained in the food, and aid the body's enzymes during digestion. The three principle enzymes produced by the body for the digestion of protein are *hydrochloric acid* and *pepsin* in the stomach, and *trypsin* secreted by the pancreas into the small intestine. [13]

− AT THE FIRST SOUND OF THE GURGLE −

Digestion of protein begins with the gastric juices in the stomach. Herein the hydrochloric acid (HCL) and the pepsin go to work. HCL is the chemical force that dissolves the protein into a sugary mass called proteose. If it were not for pepsin which speeds up this dissolving action, digestion would take HCL many hours due to the low temperature of the stomach. As the mass of proteose passes into the small intestine, pepsin continues to work with it, soon joined by another enzyme, a co-worker from the pancreas, *trypsin*. Trypsin further reduces the proteose to various less complex combinations of amino acids called polypeptides. [14] These peptides are subsequently stripped down by a final team of enzymes, the *peptidases*, until there is nothing left but free amino acids ready to pass through the mucous cells lining the interior of the small intestine.

From there the *villi*, small epithelial cells in the intestinal wall, transfer the liberated amino acids into the blood stream which carries them to the liver. Hydrolysis— that is, digestion— the first part of the energy transformation is over, and metabolism, the next step in the maturing of the amino acid, is about to begin. In chart form, the digestion of protein[15] looks like this (Fig. 3):

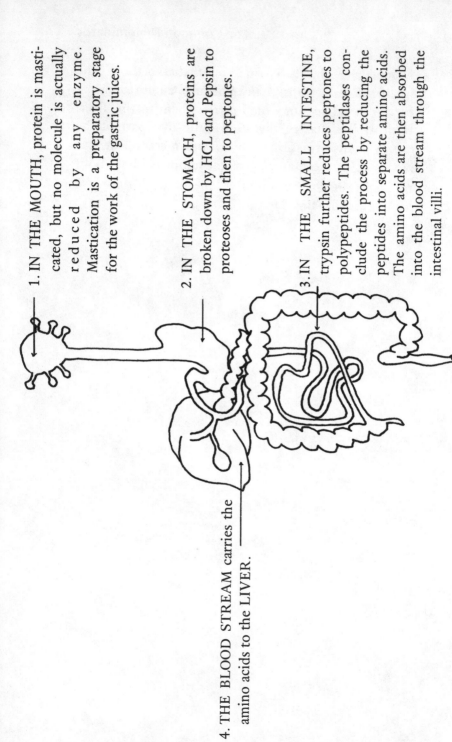

1. IN THE MOUTH, protein is masticated, but no molecule is actually reduced by any enzyme. Mastication is a preparatory stage for the work of the gastric juices.

2. IN THE STOMACH, proteins are broken down by HCL and Pepsin to proteoses and then to peptones.

3. IN THE SMALL INTESTINE, trypsin further reduces peptones to polypeptides. The peptidases conclude the process by reducing the peptides into separate amino acids. The amino acids are then absorbed into the blood stream through the intestinal villi.

4. THE BLOOD STREAM carries the amino acids to the LIVER.

FIG. 3: Summary of the Digestion of Protein: How the Body Releases Amino Acids from Protein Food.

— THE SECOND STAGE:
GETTING AN ARCHITECT TO REBUILD —

Food has supplied the raw materials. The body now supplies an architect and a blueprint: The blueprint is found in the genes. The architect is that tireless clearing agent of the body, the liver. Its handling and distribution of amino acids is only part of its heavy responsibility in maintaining critical bodily functions. In its efforts to conserve its energy in case of emergency, *the liver only allows one-fourth of itself to work at any one time.* A complete list of its daily activities is beyond the scope of this book, but in these first three chapters we shall be examining its functions in regard to amino acids from protein, fatty acids from fats, and glucose from carbohydrates. First, the newly liberated amino acids.

As the liver removes the amino acids from the blood, it has to make any of three decisions about their future. It must decide how many to store in order to make hormones, enzymes, and co-enzymes be used later; which ones will be sent back to the blood to form plasma protein— serum globulin and serum albumen [16] — and still what others will be distributed to the various cells and tissues that need repair and rebuilding. In these various undertakings the amino acid reaches its highest level of maturity. It is converted into new body protein, and enters the cell to become its chief source of life. And then, cells become tissues, tissues become organs, and organs become bodies.

The amino acid as new body protein lives and

works for approximately 120 days, the amount of time constituting the life cycle of most cells. After 120 days, younger amino acids build a new cell to take the place of the old one. The old amino acids return with other remnants of the cell to the liver to be converted into waste products and sent on to the kidneys for eventual excretion. [17]

When you think of how many cells there are, and how this constant converting, distributing, reconverting action performed on amino acids is only one of hundreds of daily operations faithfully carried out by the liver, our appreciation of this remarkable organ deepens. It is important that increased respect take the form of better care by not overloading the liver or congesting it, not simply with the wrong kinds of foods, but, as we have said, with excessive amounts of the right kinds as well.

In summary, protein metabolism takes this shape: [18], [19]

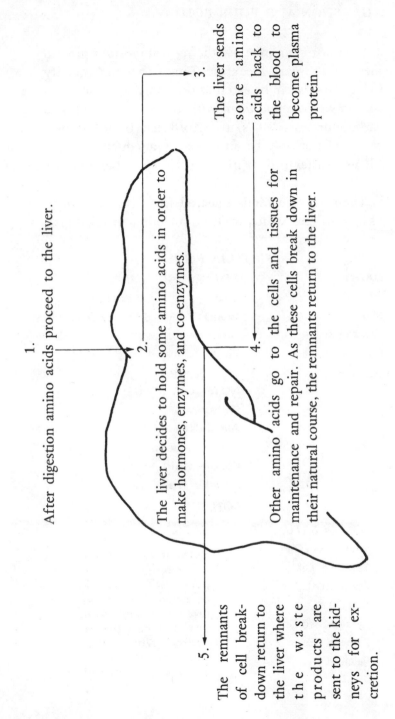

1.
After digestion amino acids proceed to the liver.

2.
The liver decides to hold some amino acids in order to make hormones, enzymes, and co-enzymes.

3.
The liver sends some amino acids back to the blood to become plasma protein.

4.
Other amino acids go to the cells and tissues for maintenance and repair. As these cells break down in their natural course, the remnants return to the liver.

5.
The remnants of cell breakdown return to the liver where the waste products are sent to the kidneys for excretion.

FIG. 4: The Metabolism of Amino Acids: How the Liver Distributes and Provides for the Body.

We must examine now the most important protein meal of the day, breakfast. First, what high quality protein foods can be eaten at breakfast, and then how should we combine them with the necessary oils and carbohydrates (CHO's) to afford us a balanced meal that will not only be nutritionally adequate but will fill us satisfactorily without stuffing or bloating us?

These are the foods selected from the first three basic nutrients which we'll be including at breakfast:

PROTEIN FOODS

DAIRY:	FISH:	MEAT:
Eggs	Sole	Lean beef patty
Milk	Flounder	Turkey patty
Yogurt	Haddock	
Cottage Cheese	Perch	

NUTS AND SEEDS:
(Pulverized)
Almonds
Sunflower seeds
Sesame seeds
Pumpkin seeds

OILS

POLYUNSATURATED:	SATURATED:
Wheat germ Oil	Butter if served, should be mixed with any polyunsaturated oil in column one. Blend 1 lb. raw butter with ½ pt. oil at room temperature. Whip until smooth. Refrigerate and use when desired.
Safflower Oil	
Sunflower Oil	
Soy Oil	
Sesame Seed Oil	
Almond Oil	
Peanut Oil	

CARBOHYDRATES

Fresh fruit, stewed fruit
Whole grain breads
Whole grain muffins and biscuits
Whole grain cereals: oatmeal and granola
Honey

— THAT INCONTROVERTIBLE LAW AGAIN —

All three types of food must be balanced at each meal; otherwise, *our natural body hunger will not be assuaged, and we will feel an emptiness from the missing ingredient, if protein, oils, and carbohydrates are not included together at each meal.* Just as we have seen that protein fulfills the cell's need for maintenance and repair, so in the following chapters we will see how the oils and carbohydrates, supplementing them, fulfill their separate functions in the body. In this chapter we are including proteins, oils, and carbohydrates as integral parts of a balanced breakfast.

One important item before we discuss the menus. The United States Department of Agriculture and the National Research Council recommends an adult daily allowance of 70 grams of protein daily,[20] although due to *individual biochemical differences*, many people burn up considerably more energy, and therefore they need more protein. Just remember that for every two pounds of body weight, we require approximately one gram of protein daily. Whatever the necessary amount may be, and we want to stress this, each of us should take the time to sit down and figure out just how much protein he is actually getting per meal. For minimum essential protein intake we should aim at approximately 20 grams per meal. Breakfast is the most important meal because the digestion of our food from the night before is thoroughly completed and what we eat in the morning has to hold many of us for four to six hours. It is good, therefore, to include an extra five to ten grams of protein at breakfast whenever possible. The protein portions listed in the following menus — and in some cases, recipes, — average approximately a 20-30 gram portion of protein food, except in cases where we have combined protein foods to provide a heartier number of grams.

THE BALANCED BREAKFAST

MENU 1. THE BREAKFAST DRINK
One or two raw fertile eggs.
One cup fruit juice (your choice) or one cup raw certified milk.
One heaping Tbsp. Lecithin granules.
One or two Tbsps. natural food protein powder.
Pinch vanilla flavoring, if desired.
Honey to sweeten according to taste.
One Tbsp. Wheat Germ Oil.
Approx. 22 grams protein.

COMMENT:

If you want to combine milk and fruit juice, use ½ cup of juice to ½ cup of milk (raw certified, if available). By a *natural food protein powder* we refer to a protein supplement which contains natural raw foods with their enzymes, and one which is possibly enriched with chelated minerals, especially calcium and magnesium— remember we said that protein and minerals should be taken together. If no such protein powder is available to you, the next alternative would be a protein supplement with papaya or pineapple enzymes added. *Enzymatic action is essential in the digestion of any food, and you always want to complement the activity of the gastric juices with the enzymes in food.* Beware of protein powders that state excessively high percentages of protein. Unless the labels are dishonest about such percentages, there seems to be little room left in the supplement for enzymes.

Don't neglect the Tbsp. of oil. If Wheat germ oil is too strong for you, either mix it with a little safflower oil, or substitute altogether the same amount of another polyunsaturated oil selected from the list of oils mentioned earlier. For reasons we will discuss in the next chapter, crude germ oils, such as the wheat germ oil, should be taken in some form during the day. If the liquid form is totally unappealing, then you should by all means substitute crude germ oil capsules.

The first menu is a perfectly balanced meal, ideal for those who don't like to eat anything in the morning but don't mind a hearty drink. As a food, it

can be further enriched with moderate amounts of
food supplements such as a Tbsp. of yeast — any
number of kinds that appeal to your taste including
those reinforced with vitamins and minerals — or a
Tbsp. of skim milk powder which not only adds
valuable protein, but a pleasant frothiness as well; or
in some parts of the country there is available a carob
flavored powder that contains time-released vitamins,
chelated minerals, hydrolyzed protein, and numerous
food synergists which aid assimilation. Such food
supplements can be added either regularly or
periodically as you see fit.

MENU 2.
*A glass of fruit juice or piece of
fresh fruit.
A Cottage cheese omelet.
Approx. 32 grams of protein.*

COMMENT:
   This is a marvelously light breakfast high in protein
value and balanced with carbohydrates in the form of
fruit or fruit juice. Although oils are used in the
preparation of the omelet, it is well always to
supplement these oils with two or three crude germ
oil capsules which give you the *raw cold pressed oils
to balance whatever hydrogenation occurs in the
other oils as they cook.*

   To prepare the cottage cheese omelet, beat up two
eggs, and place them in a Teflon pan to avoid using
oils or fats. Be sure the pan is a tough quality Teflon
such as found in T-FAL (trademark) utensils. Fry
lightly on a low heat until eggs are ready to fold; then

fold in ½ cup of cottage cheese (20 grams of protein) and cook not longer than two minutes.

Or, another way: beat up the eggs and the cottage cheese together, either whipping them in a blender or churning with an egg beater. Scramble, again avoiding additional use of oils or fats. You'll have to constantly churn them with a fork, however, so they won't stick. As a variation on this breakfast menu, instead of the cottage cheese, substitute 1 Tbsp. of the protein powder used in MENU 1, mixing it with the eggs in a blender.

As a lunch or an evening dish, chopped green onion, mushroom, celery and green pepper may be added for that extra zip and additional carbohydrate nutrition. If any cheese other than cottage cheese is used in the omelet, it should be eaten early in the day. Remember, other cheeses boost the fat content and add little protein. No other cheese comes close to the high level protein contained in cottage cheese.

> MENU 3.
> *A glass of fruit juice or a piece of fresh fruit.*
> *Two soft boiled eggs, mixed with 1 Tbsp. Almond oil.*
> *Nutseed meal toast.*
> *One eight oz. glass of milk, non-fat, whole, or buttermilk, or one cup of plain yogurt.*
> *Approx. 20 grams of protein.*

COMMENT:

Mark well that Tbsp. of almond oil. This is a light breakfast, and the hunger pangs might well arrive about mid morning if the oil is not included at breakfast. You need not restrict yourself to almond oil. Any of the polyunsaturated oils will do.

Almost everyone who tries these first three balanced breakfasts wants to add at one time or another that staple of the American breakfast, toast. Fine, but let's not make it a predominately carbohydrate addition. If we include it, we should make it a perfectly balanced food addition. Here's how:

Toast a slice of soya or whole wheat bread. Soya bread is preferable because it is higher in protein. When it is crisp and brown, butter it (with a combination of unsalted butter and raw polyunsaturated safflower oil, described on p. 34) and spread stewed fruit or fruit preserves on top. Then sprinkle a combination of pulverized almonds, sunflower seeds, sesame seeds, and pumpkin seeds on top. It is truly tasty and you've combined balanced oils, quality protein, and good carbohydrate nutrition.

This nutseed meal combination, of course, is prepared beforehand. All you need is an inexpensive electric nut grinder and raw almonds, hulled sunflower and sesame seeds (without salt), and pumpkin seeds. Place a small quantity of each in the grinder and spin them until they make a fine meal. Mix all four together in a bowl and store in the refrigerator. This tasty nut-seed combination used in a variety of ways adds extra flavor and balanced nutrition to any meal. Add it to hot or cold cereals, sprinkle it on fruit or salads, mix it with meat to make patties or loaves, add it to breading for fish and poultry. It might even be used as a balanced breakfast snack by itself:

MENU 4.
A glass of fruit juice, or a piece of stewed or fresh fruit.
1-2 slices of nut-seed toast.
Approx. 5-7 grams protein per slice.

COMMENT:

This snack, though it is balanced with the three basic nutrients, does not reach the recommended protein level of twenty grams. Adding the breakfast drink from Menu 1, however, will raise the protein to the twenty gram level, even without protein powder, if milk is used.

Caution: Starches and concentrated sugars (not fruit) combined with cholesterol foods may hold cholesterol in the blood, *if an individual has this biochemical tendency.* Such individuals, therefore, should not use the previous Menu 3, or combine Menu 4 with eggs or *any* animal protein. Others without the tendency, however, may proceed with discretion.

Raw or toasted nut butters such as almond and peanut butters, if tolerated by the liver, make excellent protein and oil spreads on your morning toast. Each Tbsp. gives approximately four grams of protein. Such butters go well with fresh fruit, such as apple or banana.

MENU 5. THE HEARTY MAN'S BREAK-
FAST

*A glass of fruit juice, or a piece
of fresh or stewed fruit.*

*Two eggs, soft boiled or
scrambled.*

One lean beef or turkey patty.

*Nutseed toast as above, if de-
sired.*

Without toast: approx. 30 grams of protein.

With toast: approx. 35-37 grams of protein.

COMMENT:

3-3½ oz. lean beef patties may be prepared ahead
of time and frozen. When making the patties, mix a
generous amount of the nut-seed meal with the meat.
This not only gives the meat a delicious flavor and a
firmer texture, but also increases the protein content
and helps balance the saturated fat in the beef.

MENU 6. (A variation of Menu 5.)

*A glass of fruit juice, or a piece
of fresh or stewed fruit.*

One or two eggs soft boiled.

Fillet of sole, perch, or halibut.

Nutseed toast if desired.

Without toast: approx. 30 grams of protein.

With toast: 35-37 grams of protein approx.

COMMENT:

The 3-3½ oz. fillet may be either broiled or fried,
though we recommend the broiling method. If you
choose to fry it, bread it in soy flour and fry it lightly

in a small amount of butter, or in a Teflon pan. One
minute on each side.

MENU 7.
*Fresh fruit combination or
stewed fruit, sprinkled generously with nutseed meal, approx. 2
heaping Tbsps.*
*½ cup of cottage cheese, or 1 cup
plain yogurt (8 grams of protein
only).*

COMMENT:

   This breakfast when eaten with the yogurt does
not reach the 20 gram protein level. This can be
remedied by combining in a blender the cup of plain
yogurt and one raw egg. For a change of flavor, add a
drop or two of strawberry or any fruit concentrate,
or vanilla extract.

MENU 7. with cottage cheese, 25-27 grams
of protein; with yogurt, 13-15 grams of
protein.

CEREAL AT BREAKFAST

MENU 8 (a)
Fruit juice, if desired.
*A bowl of cereal, one of the
natural grain varieties, with milk,
honey, sliced fruit if desired.*

*The breakfast drink from Menu
1. Approx. 25-30 grams of
protein.*

COMMENT:

Remember, any raw cereal, no matter how much protein is advertised on the label, is higher in carbohydrate content than in protein content. You would have to eat an excessive amount of the cereal to get from it the 20 grams of breakfast protein. About the only cereal that would come close would be wheat germ, one cup of which contains 17 grams of protein,[21] and wheat germ is the only raw cereal with that high a protein content per cup. The breakfast drink from Menu 1 completes the protein recommendation. And don't neglect to include the wheat germ oil; otherwise, the only oils you'll be getting at breakfast will be from the seeds and nuts in the cereal which is not sufficient to keep away that midmorning hunger.

MENU 8 (b)

A glass of fruit juice.
A bowl of natural grain cereal with an egg and milk combination.
Sprinkle cereal with 1 heaping Tbsp. of natural food protein powder, add honey if desired.

Top with sliced fruit dipped generously in the nutseed meal.
Approx. 20 grams of protein.

COMMENT:

The egg and milk combination helps boost the fat-protein content of the breakfast. Simply beat one egg into the ¾ cup of milk before pouring it over the cereal. The protein powder may be added then also. The nut-seed meal also boosts the protein, but more importantly, it balances the oils.

MENU 9. A SPECIAL OATMEAL/CREAM OF RYE RECIPE

INGREDIENTS FOR A SINGLE SERVING:
¼ cup rolled oats, cream of rye or seven grain cereal.
1 Tbsp. presoaked raisins.
1 tsp. Lecithin granules.
1 tsp. polyunsaturated oil.
1 Tbsp. Nutseed Meal.
1 raw fertile egg.
½ cup water.
1 Tbsp. Honey.
Pinch salt.

DIRECTIONS: Beat well or mix in blender the egg and lecithin granules. Set aside. Place in a pot or a double boiler the rolled oats or the rye, water and presoaked raisins. Add blended mixture of egg and lecithin. Bring to a boil. Cook until nearly ready to serve. Just before serving, stir in oil, nutseed meal, honey, and add salt. Serve, adding a little milk and more honey if desired. For extra bulk, add 1 Tbsp. of natural bran, a very important addition for efficient elimination. This makes a well-rounded, hearty breakfast, but if you're still hungry, here's the starving man's breakfast:

MENU 10.

> *A glass of fruit juice.*
> *Special oatmeal recipe, or the granola type cereal from Menu 8 (a).*
> *Two eggs, soft boiled or scrambled.*
> *3 oz. broiled lean beef patty or fish.*

COMMENT:

This is an extremely heavy meal, and its choice should be governed by natural hunger. Remember, too much nutrition, even from well-balanced sources, is just as dangerous as not enough.

PROTEIN REVIEW:
SOME TIPS THAT MAKE A DIFFERENCE

1) To find what your daily minimum protein intake should be, divide your weight by two. Spread out your daily intake so that at the end of the day you will have taken in approx. that much protein.

2) Always center each meal around a complete protein food, and only then consider the incomplete proteins as supplements.

3) Balance protein with polyunsaturated oils and carbohydrates from either fruits, vegetables, or grains at each meal.

4) Keep digestive and metabolic pathways clear by insuring a good supply of hydrochloric acid and pepsin in the stomach.

CHAPTER THREE:

THE MOST ABUSED NUTRIENT IN OUR DIETS

Though carbon, hydrogen, and oxygen exist in every food we eat, there are certain foods in which the combination of these three elements are linked in the same ratio as they are in water. These foods are called carbohydrates. Hundreds of foods including apples, table sugar, and potatoes are formally classified as carbohydrates, or saccharides, i.e., sugars. There are basically three generations of sugars in the saccharide family:[1]

Polysaccharides (poly= many)
Disaccharides (di= twice one)
Monosaccharides (mono= one)

The polysaccharide is the most complex sugar in the family, taking different forms in various members of the vegetable kingdom. In vegetables such as rice and potatoes, it is commonly identified as starch; while in celery and lettuce it is known as cellulose. The firmly linked combinations of carbon, hydrogen, and oxygen in polysaccharides makes this sugar too tough to pass immediately into the blood stream without first becoming less complicated in a disaccharide form.[2] As we shall see in more detail later, any polysaccharide must re-emerge in the second generation form of maltose, a disaccharide nearly identical to its sister sucrose, table sugar, or its brother lactose, milk sugar.[3] Any of these disaccharides going through the digestive process, though they are simpler in structure than the polysaccharides, must become simpler yet in order to get into the blood stream. They must emerge in still a third generation, the monosaccharides. The monosaccharide is pure energy. In fruit it is called fructose; in the intestines as digested milk sugar, galactose; and in the blood stream, glucose.[4] Glucose is the monosaccharide with the magic combination of atoms without which we would simply collapse on the spot: $C_6H_{12}O_6$.

Glucose, or blood sugar as it is sometimes referred to, must remain at a certain level in the blood stream. To accomplish a stability in blood sugar, the body employs a group of cells in the pancreas called the

Isles of Langerhans which reacts to a chain command of stimulation originating in the gluco-receptor mechanism in the brain. The impulses travel from there to the pituitary gland, to the adrenals, the liver, and finally the pancreas which regulates the level of glucose in the blood stream. When the blood level glucose gets too high, the gluco-receptor in the brain and the pituitary gland stimulate the liver and the pancreas to secrete insulin into the blood stream to bring the blood sugar down to where it belongs. Unbalanced carbohydrate nutrition is one of the major causes of the insulin mechanism wearing out, for if the blood sugar is constantly shooting upward, that mechanism has to work more frequently to return it to normal. It is when blood sugar gets below normal, that the stomach contracts, and we get what we commonly refer to as the hungry feeling. It is time, the body is telling us, to refuel, for that is what glucose is — fuel. Just how the polysaccharides are reduced to the monosaccharide state and how they get to the liver to be released as fuel constitutes the drama of carbohydrate-into-energy.

— NO MAN'S MEAT, EVERY MAN'S POISON —

The foods that contribute substantial high quality carbohydrate nutrition include the following:

FRUITS
VEGETABLES
WHOLE GRAIN BREADS, CRACKERS, BISCUITS
WHOLE GRAIN CEREALS
NUTS, SEEDS, LEGUMES

We must eliminate concentrated carbohydrates which contain excessive concentrated amounts of sugar that overload the blood stream with glucose, for example:

> *Candy, with 4-6 tsps. granulated sugar per piece.*
> *Cookies, with 1½ tsp. granulated sugar each.*
> *Pies, with 7-10 tsps. granulated sugar per slice.*
> *Ice cream, with 5-7 tsps. per scoop.*
> *Cake, with 5-10 tsps. per slice.*
> *Sherbert, with 9 tsps. per ½ cup.*
> *Soft drinks, with a wide range of sugar content, anywhere from 1½-9 tsps. of granulated sugar per 12 oz. bottle.*

Such sweet sorrows contain not only the white sugar which leeches the B vitamin from the system, but also artificial preservatives which make the liver toxic and which irritate the mucous lining in the intestines. It is far better for our nutrition to adhere to the natural carbohydrate foods listed above for a consistent source of easily used carbohydrates. If you buy confections and bakery goods free from preservatives and made with honey, it is advisable to eat them in small amounts, serving them only occasionally, however, and not regularly.

There are three acts to the Carbohydrate-to-Energy drama. As a prelude let's look at the set for Act One.

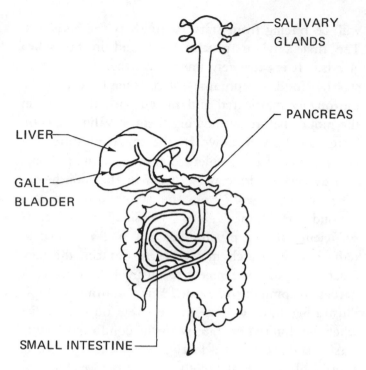

SALIVARY
GLANDS

PANCREAS

LIVER

GALL
BLADDER

SMALL INTESTINE

FIG. 5:   Organs Directly Involved with Carbohydrate Digestion.

Each of these organs, of course, contributes a specific enzyme or group of enzymes to the breaking down of the carbohydrate from the tough polysaccharide ancestor buried in food to the simple monosaccharide base newly delivered into the blood stream.

– ACT ONE, SCENE ONE: THE MOUTH –

Recall in the last chapter that the names of enzymes are recognizable from the suffix -ase or -in. The group name for the enzyme family working on starch, one of the major polysaccharides, and one we will be tracing from start to finish is the *amylases*. The first amylase, ptyalin, is found in the saliva glands.[5] It is extremely important, therefore that all starchy foods — potatoes, rice, bread, corn — be thoroughly masticated and mixed with the saliva in the mouth before swallowing them. Ptyalin works on starch all the way down to the small intestine, but never forget that complete digestion of the polysaccharide carbohydrate must begin in the mouth. No other enzyme works on the starch until it goes beyond the stomach into the small intestine. If sufficient salivary ptyalin has not had a chance to reduce initial starch molecules to dextrin, the pancreatic enzyme that meets it later will have to work harder to complete digestion. This is another example illustrating how we put undue stress on our bodies when we don't cooperate with the conditions Nature has established. Neglecting to chew starches thoroughly is one of the common ways we abuse the food value of the carbohydrate, and cheat our bodies out of its nutrition.

Ideally, by the time a polysaccharide reaches the small intestine it has changed from starch to dextrin or nearly so. The pancreatic amylase, amylopsin, secreted into the small intestine is ready either to complete the change of starch to dextrin or to initiate the changing of dextrin into maltose. As a disaccharide form, maltose passes into the lower third of the small intestine, and the last enzyme, maltase, goes into action to reduce the maltose to glucose.[6] This completes the transition from polysaccharide to monosaccharide. Glucose empties immediately into the blood stream where it is carried directly to the liver.

We did mention briefly another polysaccharide, cellulose. There is no enzyme in the body to break down cellulose; in other words, no cellulase.[7] The colon will eventually use the minute bits of cellulose broken up by the teeth in chewing as a broom to sweep the waste products of digested food out through the anal passage.[8] If cellulose, such as found in lettuce, celery, radishes, cucumbers, etc., is not broken up thoroughly, it can have just the opposite effect in the digestive tract. Blockages will occur, causing gas, putrefaction, and bloating.[9] So remember, — and this is another of those conditions Nature sets down for us and expects us to recognize and follow — since you can't break cellulose *down* in digestion, make sure you always break it *up* before swallowing.

We have traced the digestion of starch, a member of the polysaccharide family which requires the use of many carbohydrate enzymes. Not all carbohydrates, however, require that much digestion. Fruit and honey, two carbohydrate foods of the simpler monosaccharide family, need no enzymatic conversion, since their sugar can pass directly into the blood stream through the intestinal wall. Milk and table sugar, two members of the disaccharide family (di= twice the *mono*saccharide combination of carbon, hydrogen, and oxygen), need the activity of only two enzymes in the small intestine. For sucrose (table sugar), sucr*ase*; and for lactose (milk sugar), lact*ase*.

The immediate product is glucose.

To summarize, let's chart what has taken place in the digestion of carbohydrates, Act One of our threefold drama:

CARBOHYDRATES INTO ENERGY
SUMMARY OF EVENTS IN ACT ONE: *DIGESTION*

CAST OF CHARACTERS:

THE SACCHARIDE (SUGAR) FAMILY TREE:

MONOSACCHARIDES	DISACCHARIDES	POLYSACCHARIDES
(Simple sugars: $C_6H_{12}O_6$)	(Twice as tough as the Monosaccharides: $C_{12}H_{22}O_{11}$)	(Many times tougher than the others: $C_6H_{10}O_5$)
Glucose	Sucrose	Starch
Fructose	Lactose	Dextrin
Galactose	Maltose	Cellulose

(continued)

Each type of carbohydrate has its special enzyme which produces a by-product which becomes part of a chain ending in glucose:

ENZYME	DIGESTS	PRODUCES
Salivary amylase: Ptyalin	STARCH	DEXTRIN
Pancreatic amylase: Amylopsin	STARCH & DEXTRIN	MALTOSE
Sucrase	SUCROSE	GLUCOSE
Maltase	MALTOSE	GLUCOSE
Lactase	LACTOSE	GLUCOSE
(Intestinal enzymes)		& GALAC-TOSE

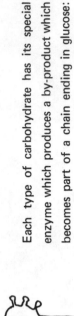

1. Carbohydrates enter the mouth. If starch is present, the salivary enzyme, ptyalin, mixes well with it. If no starch is present, the carbohydrate proceeds unaffected down through the stomach into the small intestine. The starch, meanwhile, is converted into dextrin by the ptyalin.

2. The pancreas secretes amylopsin into the small intestine. Amylopsin completes the conversion of starch to dextrin and goes on to convert dextrin to maltose.

3. The last enzyme, maltase, reduces the maltose to glucose which passes readily through the intestinal wall into the blood stream. Likewise, other disaccharide enzymes, sucrase and lactase will reduce sucrose and lactose respectively to glucose.

FIG. 6: Summary of the Digestion of Starch and other Carbohydrates: How the Body Releases Glucose from Carbohydrate Food.

— ACT TWO: HOW THE LIVER GETS
GLUCOSE TO THE CELLS —

After the digestion of glucose, the blood stream carries it to the liver which does one of two things. It either returns the glucose to the blood stream where it is needed for energy, or it stores it for future use. And here, one of nature's delicate, marvelously economical operations takes place. The liver would obviously be able to store more energy for the future if glucose were not so bulky. So, instead of accumulating energy in the form of $C_6H_{12}O_6$, it condenses glucose by removing from it one molecule of water (H_2O) for use elsewhere in the body. The result is an economical $C_6H_{10}O_5$ or *glycogen.* When energy in its original form of glucose is needed in the blood stream, the liver will replace the molecule of water, converting glycogen back to glucose so the other cells in the body will be able to utilize it.[11] This remarkable principle of the body's economy, called *glycolysis*, represents both the beginning and the end of a fascinating energy-transformation cycle.

— THAT BUSY ARCHITECT AGAIN —

First, the liver sends glucose through the blood stream to all the cells. These cells, of course, include the muscles. Once we understand the unique roll muscles play in the conversion of energy, we can easily resolve many otherwise unexplained problems in the daily functioning of our muscles.

Other than the liver, the muscles are the only tissues able to convert large amounts of glucose into glycogen. They store glycogen until the muscles require its conversion to glucose for burning. At that time, the adrenal glands and the pancreas join forces to support the muscles. They donate respectively two hormones, adrenalin (epinephrine) and glucagon, which trigger a specific muscle enzyme to reconvert glycogen to glucose. The glucose is then burned for energy, leaving behind a series of by-products. One of these, lactic acid, returns to the liver and is recycled as glycogen. [12] The body, you see, wastes nothing; any element that can be used productively is recycled into new activity. In terms of ecology, we have been a long time learning this lesson from nature, and we may pay for it dearly if we do not follow her example more conscientiously. The best examples of how to treat our planetary environment are found right within the more immediate environment of our own bodies.

Act Two's cycle continues, daily, hourly: [13]

ACT TWO:

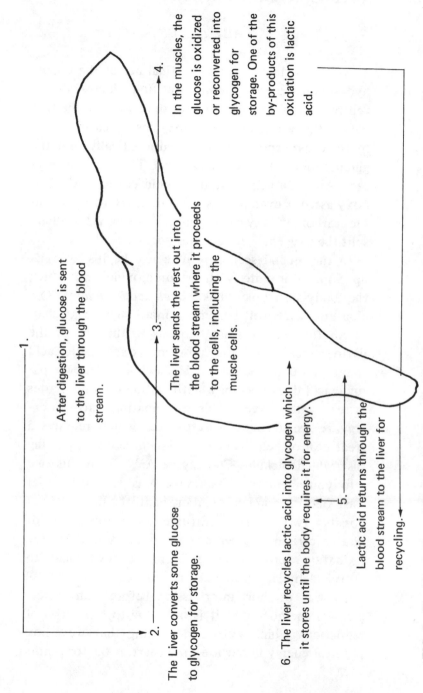

After digestion, glucose is sent to the liver through the blood stream.

The Liver converts some glucose to glycogen for storage.

The liver sends the rest out into the blood stream where it proceeds to the cells, including the muscle cells.

In the muscles, the glucose is oxidized or reconverted into glycogen for storage. One of the by-products of this oxidation is lactic acid.

6. The liver recycles lactic acid into glycogen which it stores until the body requires it for energy.

Lactic acid returns through the blood stream to the liver for recycling.

FIG. 7: The Metabolism of Glucose, Part One: How the Liver Gets Glucose to the Cells and Recycles Waste Products.

– *ACT THREE* –

As the curtain rises on the final act of the Carbo-hydrate-into-Energy drama, we find glucose in the cell ready for the first stages of oxidation. In the first scene, three microprotein enzymes – carboxylase, hydrogenase, and oxygenase – dramatically split the glucose molecule into many parts. The enzymes proceed with the help of non- protein co-enzymes. Carboxylase, for example, uses Vitamin B1 to help split the carbon;[14] oxygenase uses Vitamin B2 to help split the oxygen;[15] it becomes pyruvic acid.

In the second scene, pyruvic acid begins to break up. Some of it unites with carbon dioxide from which the body's enzymes make *oxaloacetic acid.*[17] Oxaloacetic acid will become a more significant character after we see what happens to the rest of the pyruvic acid. For the moment, oxaloacetic acid stands aside in the wings. Meanwhile, whatever pyruvic acid does not unite with carbon dioxide, unites instead with oxygen. This combination starts an energy releasing (oxidation) process which requires a great deal of help from a multi-membered supporting cast which includes Co-enzyme A.[18] Burn this one into your memory; Co-enzyme A is derived from at least one B-Complex member, pantothenic acid (and possibly two others).[19'] Situated on a foundation of double carbon fragments, co-enzyme A initiates the oxidation process by reducing pyruvic acid to acetylaldehyde.[20] (cf. chart, p. 63)

By way of short intermission before scene three, please remember that it is only due to this series of reductions which we are describing that we enjoy physical energy in our life. (see chart, p. 63, for points of energy release); that is, we *should be,* unless somewhere along the way a breakdown in the cycle occurs. Fatigue, for example, might occur from the accumulation of acetylaldehyde since this by-product is chemically related to formaldehyde.[21] In this case, particularly, a lack of B12 leaves one feeling sluggish, sleepy, and toxic. However, with B12's support, co-enzyme A will further reduce acetylaldehyde by combining with it, knocking out the aldehyde, and leaving just the acetyl and itself. This new character is called Acetylcoenzyme A.[22]

The attachment between Co-enyme A and Acetyl is short lived. In scene three, they split apart. Co-enzyme departs, returns to an old friend, pyruvic acid, and goes about, once again, to reduce pyruvic acid into acetylaldehyde — a necessary rut of sorts. Meanwhile, the acetyl fraction links with oxaloacetic acid, and the result of this is the birth of the Citric Acid Cycle.

Citric acid is so important, it has an entire cycle named after it. Since citric acid wants nothing more than to be reconverted into one of its parent substances, the citric acid cycle recycles citric acid into a character we thought we had seen the last of — oxaloacetic acid. It takes a quick change artist such as citric acid to execute a bravura series of lightning fast oxidations and reductions[24] (citric into isocitric, into ketoglutaric, into succinic, into fumaric, into malic) until it rearranges itself into the once more recognizable oxaloacetic acid. Oxaloacetic acid continues about its business, determined, it seems, to keep the cycle going by forever linking with more acetyl coenzyme A, and so forth, as described in the figure opposite this page.

You see, we cannot minimize the importance of oxaloacetic acid. Though virtually unknown by most people, its inadequacy occasions ketosis, a build up of acetone and other ketone bodies,[25,26] and eventually an impaired carbohydrate tolerance appears, which might well take the form of hypoglycemia or diabetes.[27]

Just when we think the drama is over, the curtain rises briefly for an epilogue. We visit pyruvic acid, which we have seen converted by co-enzyme A into acetylaldehyde. However, not all of the pyruvic acid is converted. A portion of it is drained off to become another by-product called lactic acid which diffuses easily into bodily fluids. Although the heart can re-convert lactic acid into pyruvic acid to be burned for energy, any build-up of lactic acid in the tissues will become toxic to the muscles and must be further broken down by enzymes and co-enzymes such as pantothenic acid and para-amino-benzoic acid. Exercise is most important in this regard, for though niacin and the other two vitamins just mentioned work to reconvert lactic into pyruvic,[28,29] it is foremost the use of regular exercise which helps the body to rid itself of accumulated lactic acid. Just as lactic acid accumulates, so does the pyruvic acid as well. And just as lactic acid can be the cause of muscle soreness and tightening, so a widespread accumulation of pyruvic acid in the system can irritate the nerves and become the source of nervous tension.

With this warning, the curtain falls on the Carbo-hydrate-into-Energy drama. As we leave for lunch, a summary-at-a-glance diagram affords us an instant replay of the drama, on display in Figure 8.

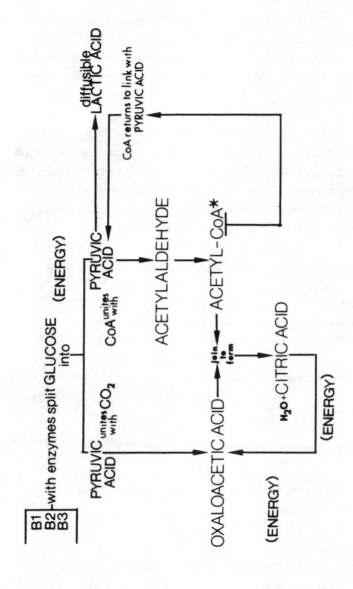

FIG. 8: The Metabolism of Glucose, Part Two: How the Cells Make Energy Out of Glucose.

— PLANNING THE NUTRITIONAL LUNCH —

As we go through our luncheon menus, we must keep in mind our PROTEIN-OIL-CARBOHYDRATE priority. Though we have analysed carbohydrates in this chapter, when it comes to selecting food for a balanced meal, we must not forget to center our nutrients around a twenty to thirty gram portion of protein, supplemented with one to two Tbsp. of polyunsaturated oil, and a generous portion of carbohydrates (3-3½ oz.) primarily from fruits or vegetables, secondarily from cereals and whole grain breads. Below are the foods selected from the three basic nutrients which we'll be dealing with at lunch:

PROTEIN FOODS

DAIRY	FISH	MEAT
Eggs	Sole	Lean hamburger
Milk	Flounder	Lean steak
Yogurt	Tuna	All beef franks
Cottage cheese	Salmon	
	Shrimp	NUTS & SEEDS (pulverized)
		Almonds
		Walnuts
		Sunflower seeds
		Sesame seeds
		Pumpkin seeds

OILS

POLYUNSATURATED:	UNSATURATED
in liquid or capsules	SALAD DRESSINGS:
as available:	

Wheat Germ Oil

Safflower Oil

Sunflower Seed Oil

Soy Oil

Sesame Seed Oil

Almond Oil

Peanut Oil

SATURATED:

Oil and Vinegar based.
Mayonnaise from
polyunsaturated oils.

LECITHIN GRANULES
OR CAPSULES

Butter, always to be
balanced with any
polyunsaturated oil
above.

Note: The pulverized seeds and nuts listed under protein foods are likewise excellent sources of poly-unsaturated oils.

CARBOHYDRATES

Fresh or steamed vegetables

Fresh or stewed fruits

Whole grain breads or crackers or rolls

Honey

Though we will be dealing explicitly with oils in the next chapter, we must give you a good rule of thumb to follow when consuming oils and fats. To insure the balance, digestion, and proper assimilation of oils in each of these menus, *always balance saturated fats with polyunsaturated oils and emulsify them with lecithin.* People for whom this rule has become second nature in eating have never regretted it.

In several of our luncheon menus, a vegetable salad is recommended to provide necessary carbohydrate nutrition. Your own blend of fresh vegetables is preferable, of course, but may we suggest that yours include some of the raw vegetables listed in either of these two luncheon salads:

SALAD #1	SALAD #2
Raw tomato slices	Romaine lettuce
Alfalfa Sprouts	Butter or Boston lettuce
	Red leaf lettuce
	Endive
	Chickory
	Sliced cucumbers
	Grated carrots
	Chopped celery

Other salad possibilities which suggest themselves to you and which you might like to substitute or add to Salads 1 & 2 can be found at the close of the next chapter. There we also caution about regulating salad according to our ability to handle cellulose.

— THE BALANCED LUNCH —

MENU 1.

Tuna salad, shrimp salad, or salmon salad blended with chopped celery, polyunsaturated oil mayonnaise, and seasoned salt.
Salad #1 or #2, with oil based dressing or lemon juice.

Whole grain wheat or soy crackers, if desired.

MENU 2.

Chicken salad or turkey salad blended with chopped celery, polyunsaturated oil mayonnaise and seasoned salt.
Salad #1 or #2 with oil based dressing or lemon juice.
Whole grain soy or wheat crackers, if desired.

COMMENT:

In either Menu 1 or 2, the oil based dressing and the crackers should be eliminated to make both menus good lunches for reducing. They are high in protein, which is desirable if overweight is a problem and you want a lunch that will help you to lose unwanted pounds.

MENU 3.

Two all beef frankfurters.
½ cup of cottage cheese.
Salad #1 or #2 with oil based dressing or lemon juice.
One whole wheat hot dog bun, if desired.
Garnish with pickles and tomatoes.

COMMENT:

The franks should either be roasted or boiled, and not fried in grease. Since there has been recent controversy in many health periodicals concerning the contamination of mustard, we advise discretion in its use as a condiment. When the bread is omitted from this menu, its high protein content makes it a good lunch for reducing. Its ingredients *are* balanced nutritionally. Recall, e.g., the rule of thumb regarding oils and fats: the polyunsaturated oil in the salad dressing is essential to balance the saturated fat in the meat.[1]

MENU 4.

Two eggs, soft or hard boiled.
A glass of milk, whole, low fat, or butter milk.
Raw tomato slices with oil based dressing, or polyunsaturated mayonnaise.

MENU 5.

Egg Salad on a large, crisp leaf of romain lettuce or on a bed of alfalfa sprouts.
Raw tomato slices with oil based dressing or lemon juice.
A glass of milk, whole, low fat, or buttermilk.

COMMENT:

For the light touch, these are standard variations on one of our earlier breakfast menus. They are good balanced meals for weight conscious people who want balanced nutrition with sufficient caloric intake. The mayonnaise in the egg salad and the oil based dressing balances the saturated fat in the egg and the milk.

MENU 6.
> *½ cup of cottage cheese with fruit salad, or with raw tomato slices.*
> *Supplement with flaxseed, safflower, or wheat germ oil capsules.*

COMMENT:

Another light lunch for those who eat heavily at breakfast or who want to lose weight. This is the first menu which requires the use of food in capsule form to efficiently supplement a polyunsaturated oil requirement. Wheat Germ Oil in liquid form, of course, will do just as well, if desired. More on the reasons for this in our next chapter.

MENU 7.   THE HEARTY MAN's LUNCH

PROTEIN: (select one:) 3½ oz. baked or broiled fillet of sole, perch, halibut, or salmon. A lean steak. A lean beef patty.
CARBOHYDRATE: (select one along with the salad) Wild rice. Salad #1 or#2. Baked potato.

OILS: Oil based salad dressing or polyunsaturated oil mayonnaise. Optional: 1 Tbsp. Safflower oil alone or mixed with butter on a baked potato.

COMMENT:

This is really a mid-day dinner, the type of meal you might eat if you have skipped breakfast or are in the habit of eating your main meal at noon. If this is the case, we must make certain qualifications. First, since it is very difficult to be certain of quality polyunsaturated oils in restaurants, it would be very wise to supplement this meal with a generous supplement of oil capsules such as we have mentioned, especially if the fish is fried instead of broiled or roasted, and if the baked potato comes with a thick patty of butter, or mixed with cheese, or topped with sour cream.

Secondly, it is best not to order cooked vegetables in a restaurant to supply carbohydrate nutrition because they are seldom fresh, usually overcooked, and have baking soda added to them during the cooking which destroys many of the nutrients. Although they may look beautiful in the dish, they are hardly worth the eating. Stick to tossed salads containing dark green leafy vegetables. Many restaurants now have smorgasbord salads, where customers can combine their own ingredients, and somewhere in the choice of dressings there should be one with a polyunsaturated oil base to supply balanced oil nutrition. If not, be sure to supplement with capsules.

MENU 8. THE LUNCH DRINK
For a complete meal, mix well in a blender the following ingredients:
One cup whole or low fat milk.
One Tbsp. natural food protein powder.
One ripe banana (skin very dark, soft inside).

One Tbsp. almond butter.
One Tbsp. honey, according to taste.
One Tbsp. skim milk powder and one egg may be added for additional protein.
Include one scoop of ice cream made from natural ingredients for an even richer treat.

COMMENT:

This is an excellent drink for anyone underweight. The rest of us should remember that the balance of nutrients in the drink will not put on extra pounds as long as the total intake of calories per day does not exceed what is burned up in the cells. We recommend that this drink, delicious as it is, be taken separately as a meal in itself, balanced perhaps with a green salad, and not be used as part of another menu. By itself, we think you will find it is quite filling and satisfying.

– FOR THE SOUP AND SANDWICH CROWD –

The last four menus go well with a bowl of hot soup, a favorite luncheon combination for many people. On a chilly day, nothing seems to hit the spot better than a steaming bowl of soup or chowder, especially if it is home made with natural ingredients, or if it is selected from among the many commercial varieties, one blessedly free, we hope, from artificial preservatives. Since most soups are starchy and thus quite filling, be sure the soup does not usurp the rightful place of the balanced protein-oil-carbohydrate priority. You may have to avoid soups altogether if further eating at the same meal amounts to overindulgence. A light beef or chicken broth might be better substituted, for it is higher in protein nutrition and lower in starch. One excellent way to boost your protein at lunch is to start off with a cup of amino acid broth. The recipe is as follows:

> *2 tsp. hydrolyzed amino acid powder or*
> *1 Tbsp. of the liquid amino acid. Mix well in one cup of boiling water.*
> *OPTIONAL: 1 tsp. vegetable broth powder, or pinch of beef bouillon.*

COMMENT:

This is not a completely balanced meal. It is rather the beginning of one, for it can supply that extra protein needed during a meal that may be low in amino acid content. Since hydrolyzed, the amino acids in the broth are already in their liberated condition, they proceed directly to the liver for distribution throughout the body. Taken as a snack in mid afternoon, new vigor is detectable almost immediately. Whenever amino acids enrich the cells, the head clears, energy returns to the body, arms and legs cease to feel heavy, and sluggishness disappears.

MENU 9.

> *Hot soup or amino acid broth.*
> *Tuna salad, chicken salad, or egg salad sandwich with raw tomato*

slices and alfalfa sprouts with polyunsaturated oil mayonnaise. On whole grain soy or wheat bread.

MENU 10.

Hot soup or amino acid broth.
Hot fish sandwich with thick slice of raw tomato and alfalfa sprouts on whole grain soy or wheat bun, with blend of poly-unsaturated oil mayonnaise and pickled relish.

COMMENT:

The selection of fish should be based on high protein content. We recommend those mentioned earlier: flounder, perch, sole, cod, halibut.

MENU 11.

Amino acid broth or hot soup.
Lean hamburger with raw onion slice and thick slice of raw tomato on whole wheat or soy bun toasted.
Salad #2 with oil based dressing.

MENU 12.

Amino acid broth, using 1 Tbsp. rather than 1 tsp.
Nut butter sandwich (peanut or almond) on soy bread toasted with fresh fruit preserves.
Salad #1 with lemon juice.

COMMENT:

This is a lunch extremely high in fats due principally to the nut butter. Nut butters always make the liver work hard, so it is essential to include the amino acid broth rather than soup or bouillon, chiefly for the methionine which aids fat metabolism in the liver. Since peanut butter sandwiches are a favorite among preteens and teen agers, we feel it is important that a lunch centered around nut butter sandwiches include additional nutrients to support the body in the metabolic process. Peanut butter alone is an incomplete protein, and it must always be supplemented with foods such as the soya or whole wheat bread, not white bread, and milk which make a complete amino acid balance. If the broth is inconvenient or unappealing, substitute the amino acid in tablet form either immediately before or after the meal. They are small and easy to carry in lunch bags or may even be tucked away in a locker or a desk drawer.

If milk is easily tolerated, an 8 oz. glass may be substituted for the broth, thus assuring complete protein intake. If milk causes indigestion and flatulence, however, don't add to the difficulty of assimilation by taking it with a nut butter sandwich. Not only is the liver strained, but the stomach enzymes, hydrochloric acid and pepsin, might likewise be drained and toxicity is likely to follow in one form or another.

— CARBOHYDRATE REVIEW —

TIPS THAT MAKE THE DIFFERENCE:

1. No meal should be centered around carbohydrates. Use carbohydrate foods as complementary servings to protein.
2. Carbohydrate nutrition should come chiefly from vegetables, fruits, and from their juices.
3. Each one of us must be the judge about eating breads and cereals from whole grain sources. If your body holds the sugar longer by turning it into fat, then cut down or omit them from your diet. Never abandon fruits and vegetables as the chief sources for carbohydrates.
4. Never eat white sugars. If sweeteners are desired, use small amounts of honey or date sugar.
5. Plan carbohydrate meals to include sufficient roughage, adding, for example a Tbsp. of bran to cereals, fruit dishes or yogurt servings.

CHAPTER FOUR:

THE MOST NEGLECTED
NUTRIENT IN OUR DIETS.

We come now to the third of the five basic
nutrients, oils, or more precisely, fatty acids. So few
people think of oils or fats as a basic nutrient, that is,
a food which their bodies absolutely cannot do
without. Yet there is abundant evidence all around us
that one of the major nutritional problems in
America is fat metabolism— pimples, dry skin, oily
skin, dandruff, overweight, liver disorders, lymphatic
congestion— all of which in many cases can be traced
to an inefficient handling of oils. To really understand why oils or fatty acids are indispensable to our
bodies, we have to start at the simplest level, the
molecule. Just as we began in Chapter One with the
protein molecule, so here we will begin by examining

the fatty acid molecule. There are two types of fatty acids, and just about everyone has heard of them: *saturated and unsaturated fatty acids.* Many people wonder what it is that "saturates" or "unsaturates" an oil, the understandable result of not grasping nutrition at the molecular level. Let's look at a molecule of fatty acid. It is composed, first of all, of a chain of carbon atoms, which we'll designate as:

-C-

Thus a chain of carbon atoms would look like this:

Notice how the carbon atom has, so to speak, two arms and two legs to connect it to other atoms. When the carbon atom is linked up to other carbons in a chain, each carbon has two arms free to latch on to other atoms such as oxygen and hydrogen:

-O- H-

As you can see, the oxygen atom has two arms

capable of latching onto other atoms or particles; whereas the hydrogen atom has only one arm. With all these arms available for linking, generally two possibilities for arrangement may occur in the carbon chain. To simplify the matter somewhat, we can diagram the two possibilities as follows:

FIRST POSSIBILITY: SECOND POSSIBILITY:

```
        H                         H
        |                         |
      H-C-H                     H-C-H
        |                         |
       -C-H                     HO-C-H
        |                         |
       -C-OH                     H-C-OH
        |                         |
     HO-C-                       H-C-H
        |                         |
      H-C-                      HO-C-H
        |                         |
      H-C-H                      H-C-H
        |                         |
        H                         H
```

In the first possibility we see that not all the carbons' arms are holding on to hydrogen or oxygen. Some are free. In the second possibility we see that all the carbons are holding on to hydrogens or oxygens. All the carbon links, in other words, in the second possibility are completely saturated with either hydrogen or oxygen. It is therefore a saturated fatty acid. In the first possibility almost all of the carbon links in the chain have at least one arm free or unsaturated. The more unsaturated carbon links in a fatty acid, the easier it is for our bodies to convert that acid into heat and energy.

— IN BALANCE LIES NATURE'S WISDOM —

This does not mean that we should do away altogether with saturated fats, only that we must always *balance* our intake of saturated fats with polyunsaturated oils. The *lipases,* enzymes working day and night to convert lipids (fats) into heat and energy, must dissolve the solid or semi-solid saturated fats into less saturated substances. Two common saturated fatty acids, stearic (found in meat fat) and butyric (found in butter), need the balance of linoleic acid (found in safflower oil) to increase the efficiency of their metabolism. You can understand then why we recommend mixing butter with safflower oil. Butter, like any other saturated fat, needs the extra arms of the polyunsaturates to make them useful. Only with open arms can they latch on to other nutrients which they can transport to the cells to do the work of body metabolism.

— AGAIN, A LITTLE HELP
FROM OUR FRIENDS —

Both saturated and unsaturated fatty acids need the help of linoleic acid, the critical fatty acid in the cycle. Just as we had to acquire eight amino acids from the outside so our bodies could manufacture the other fourteen, so must we acquire linoleic acid from the outside to complete the metabolism of the fatty acids. Nature, you see, never allows an organism to become completely autonomous. It must always require something from outside itself to complete its life functions. All those arms linking with each other demonstrate the strong propensity that permeates so small an element as our atoms to reach out and be united with something else. Oleic acid, for example, an unsaturated fat linked with many saturated fats in our food, must be converted by enzymes into linolenic and arachadonic acid. But these enzymes cannot go to work until the body acquires that one fatty acid it is unable to manufacture by itself.[1] Linoleic acid with the help of Vitamin B6 enables oleic acid to go the whole route:

$$(+B6)$$
OLEIC ------> LINOLEIC ------> LINOLENIC ------>
------> ARACHADONIC.

*— THUS, MAY THE ARACHADONIC
BE ALWAYS WITH YOU —*

Arachadonic acid is thought to be the active molecule because it is involved in reactions intimately related to fat—amino acid metabolism at the nuclear level. This is demonstrated by normal skin health, tissue growth, kidney repair, and the formation of steroid hormones.[2] We know that unsaturated fatty acids along with polysaccharides linked with amino acids are the basic constituents of strong cell walls. The critical nature of strong cell walls is apparent, for, after all, what can we say of the strength of the city if its protective walls are weak and defenseless.

Unsaturated acids are generally involved in the metabolism of cholesterol in some unexplained way[3] based on the fact that they all have those free arms that can pick up and carry whatever nutrient the body requires them to hook on to. Unfortunately, the body cannot call upon the saturated fats to put forth any more effort. Their arms are already full with hydrogen and oxygen, and if they don't find a willing polyunsaturate to give them a hand, they will just settle down as adipose tissue, tissue composed of those saturated fatty acids which have migrated and settled in such unwanted regions of the body as the mesentery section, that's the tummy area, between the stomach and the peritoneum sack.[4] This common type of overweight, then is due to a loss of balance. Our bodies cannot handle more energy than nature has determined, and we render her helpless when we do not engage her able associate from outside — unsaturated linoleic acid — to distribute this energy efficiently.

Another problem develops too. The ability of saturated fats to keep cholesterol in an emulsified state is greatly limited, if there is not enough linoleic acid and emulsifying agents in the diet. Cholesterol will stick to the arterial walls and eventually gum up the arteries so badly as to critically impair circulation. This, we know, has become a serious problem in the American diet. So much so, that people want to go to the extreme of avoiding cholesterol foods. They remain unaware that if sufficient amounts of cholesterol are not taken into the body and retained in an emulsified state, the liver will manufacture cholesterol as much as eight times faster, for we need essential cholesterol to form hormones. What we don't need are mischievous chunks of it floating around in our bloodstream clogging our arteries.

— THAT MYSTERIOUS EMULSIFIER —

Fortunately there is one fatty acid, a substance composed of choline, inositol, phosphoric acid, and stearic acid, which works faithfully with an amino acid methionine, to keep cholesterol in an emulsified state. It is called *lecithin.* Biochemically, although the basic action of inositol in lecithin is still a mystery,[5] it is suspected by reputable biochemists that inositol is the free lipotropic factor that prevents fatty deposits in the liver.[6] Other tests have shown that inositol has a marked effect in reducing the amount of cholesterol in the liver,[7] something choline is unable to do.[8] However, setting aside the problem of inositol, the astonishing documented success of lecithin in expediting fat metabolism remains a scientifically attested fact.[9]

Consider the components of lecithin as a group of assiduous workers engaged in extensive coenzymatic activity in the liver. Choline is the matriarchal leader of this group. She knows that phosphorus must, along with so many other duties, link up with some of those free arms extended to her by the lipids (fats) in order to get to other parts of the body. In the liver, then, choline will activate the synthesis of phosphorus and fats into *phospholipids.* To do this, she employs two co-worker enzymes: betaine, and methionine. Betaine is an alkaloid from beets and is also a fine liver detoxifier. Methionine is an amino acid found abundantly in eggs and sunflower seeds. Betaine and methionine, called lipotropics because they give choline the ammunition she needs to get the fats out of the liver and into their proper depots throughout the body, at all times carry with them a special combination of carbon and hydrogen (CH_3) called the methyl group. And it is only when choline requests the release of this methyl group that betaine and methionine yield and shift the CH_3 methyl group from one compound to another, so that choline can stimulate phosphorus to link with the lipids and get into other parts of the body where they are needed.[10] If the diet is insufficient in either choline or betaine and methionine, fatty deposits will accumulate in the liver simply because the fat does not have the proper conveyance for being transported through the body. This is the other half of the fat story that is rarely told. The polyunsaturated oils and the lipotropic factors are absolutely essential for losing unwanted pounds and keeping weight normal. Those extra arms of the oils will move the fats out of the depots and the lipotropics will initiate the burning process. All nature needs is a chance. Yet so many of us in one way or another deny her the full range of her ordered cycles when through ignorance or self-indulgence we handicap her exquisite work. A totally oil free diet is as dangerous a form of malnutrition as an amino or nucleic acid deficiency arising from insufficient protein. Then, too, on the other hand, too many deliberate choices of heated, saturated and hydrogenated fats without a corresponding balance of raw, polyunsaturated oils will bring liver and artery congestion and a disrupted transmethylation cycle.

— "TRANS-METHYL" - WHAT? —

Since this "transmethylation," or shifting of the methyl groups, [11] is so important, a food supplement in tablet form containing all of the lipotropics — methionine, betaine, choline, and inositol — may be taken to insure our success in handling fats and preventing fatty accumulations in the liver. [12]

Let's consider the best sources of polyunsaturated oils. They may be taken as food in grocery form, or as a food supplement in capsule form. If you take supplemental oil capsules to insure the proper balance of oils, look upon them naturally as food, not as medicine. Don't think that when you start taking food supplements in the form of tablets or capsules that food suddenly stops being food and becomes instead a drug or medicine. Our tendency to think this way, of course, is due to our association of pills with the pharmaceutical profession. The taking of food supplements demands an entirely different approach to the phenomenon of the capsule. Instead of associating capsules and tablets with medicine and illness, we must learn to associate them with food and consequently with health. Then, since we do not consider ourselves ill when at a meal we take food in the form of grocery or produce, so we should not consider ourselves ill when at the same meal we take food in the form of capsules or tablets.

SOURCES OF POLYUNSATURATED OILS:

COLD PRESSED OILS IN LIQUID FORM

Sunflower seed oil
Safflower oil
Sesame seed oil
Wheat germ oil
Soy oil
Almond oil
Peanut oil
Linseed oil
Corn oil

These quality oils may be purchased in health food stores in the same convenient quantities in which you find cooking oil in the supermarket.

COLD PRESSED OILS IN CAPSULE FORM

Wheat germ oil
Safflower oil
Crude germ oil combinations:
  wheat germ oil
  rice bran oil
  soy oil
  linseed oil

These oil capsules are available in various potencies. Except for the last three, they are usually measured in minums. It takes approximately sixty-two minums to make one teaspoon. A capsule containing oil may contain anywhere from six to twenty minums.

Up to this point, we have not stressed the

importance of the B vitamins, especially B6 in the absorption of oils, but we will be taking a thorough look at it in a later chapter when we consider the vitamins as co-enzymes. The presence of B6 in the system, or for that matter in any oil capsule formula, is included for the purpose of helping linoleic acid make its transition to arachadonic acid. This is the whole secret of eating food and taking food supplements: *Consume moderate amounts of high quality nutrients in combinations specifically formulated for maximum assimilation.*

The combination of crude oils— wheat germ oil, rice bran oil, and soy oil — is a powerful nutrient. Many people feel its energy very soon after taking just one or two capsules, and such oils are invaluable in providing precursors necessary for the manufacture of hormones. They should be supplied regularly.

Lecithin is available in three forms: granules, capsules, and liquid. An average intake of lecithin daily would amount to one or two tablespoons of the granules, or six to nine of the 1200 mg. (16 grain) capsules. The liquid is quite viscous and somewhat unpleasant to take, but a tablespoon a day would certainly be adequate if you choose to take it in this manner.

Choline, the most important ingredient of lecithin may be taken separately for the same reason that lecithin is taken. The more choline present in the liver, the more efficient the transmethylation and the phospholipid synthesis. Choline may be purchased in tablet form. There is no minimum or maximum requirement of choline which is non-toxic even in massive doses. An ideal way to take choline and its companion inositol is to consume it as part of a natural lipotropic group containing all four members of the lipotropic family— choline, inositol, betaine, and methionine. A food supplement so formulated would cost little or no more than taking choline separately, and such a combination will expedite a more efficient transmethylation. The additional influence of the B vitamins in this connection will be treated near the end of the chapter.

VARIOUS HIGH QUALITY FOOD SOURCES OF POLYUNSATURATED OILS:

FISH: Sole - Flounder - Perch - Halibut - Cod - Mackerel - Haddock - Tuna - Salmon.

LEGUMES, SEEDS, NUTS: Sunflower - Sesame - Pumpkin - Almond - Walnut - Peanut - Soy.

DRESSINGS: Salad dressings which are composed of polyunsaturated oils listed on p. 65. *

BUTTERS: Almond - Sesame - Peanut - Sunflower Seed.

*Include polyunsaturated oil mayonnaises.

THE FIRST STAGE OF FAT RELEASE

Let's now consider the digestion of the oils found in these high quality foods. Recalling our diagram of the digestive system, we'll concentrate this time on the four digestive organs which handle fats.

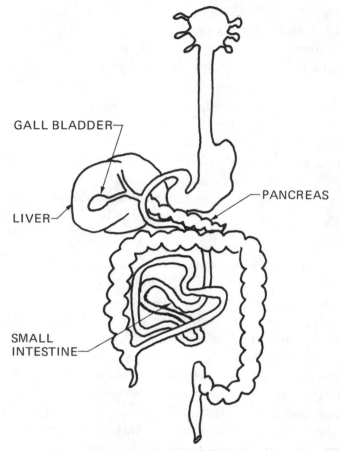

FIG. 9:   Organs Directly Involved With Fat Digestion.

One of the chief biological functions of the liver, which should come to it as naturally as breathing comes to the lungs, is the continuous manufacture and secretion of bile. Bile, composed of water, solids, bile salts, mucous, pigments, cholesterol (as well as other lipids), and inorganic salts, is not perhaps the most interesting subject of discussion, but when the liver ceases to produce it, we are in trouble. Without bile we simply cannot digest fats.[13] The liver sends some of its dark, viscous bile into the gall bladder where it is stored and made more concentrated as the walls of the gall bladder, like a sponge, absorb water from the bile. Whatever amount of bile the liver holds back from the gall bladder quite readily passes into a common duct where it is joined by the bladder bile as they move together into the small intestine. This activity is very stimulating to the pancreas, for it is this movement of bile along with the action of hydrochloric acid in the stomach that stimulates the pancreas to secrete its enzyme steapsin.[14]

Just a note on nomenclature: all fat enzymes are called *lipases,* and as we go along, you have noticed, surely, that names given to enzymes end with the letters -ase or -in, such as the lip*ase* called steaps*in*. There are many other lipases other than steapsin which take part in the body's very complicated community effort to reduce fats and oils first to free fatty acids, and then burn them up in the cells for heat and energy. It is not surprising, then, to find a whole family of enzyme co-workers trailing after steapsin into the small intestine to get to work on the fats and oils.[15]

When the fats first enter the small intestine, they are, of course, all mixed up with proteins and carbohydrates in the acid chyme freshly arrived from the stomach. Steapsin and his co-workers have to sort out the fats and oils and then free the fatty acids to mix thoroughly with the alkalies in the pancreatic and intestinal juices.[16]

— DIVORCE WITH A HAPPY ENDING —

The chain molecules of all fats and oils are composed of one part glycerine wedded to three parts fatty acid.[17] When steapsin divorces the three parts of fatty acid from the one part of glycerine, the glycerine is absorbed immediately through the intestinal villi into the lymphatic system. There they wait to be reunited with their fatty acids. And, sure enough, once the fatty acids have thoroughly mixed with the intestinal alkalies, they pass through the same villi and recombine with the glycerine to form new body fat. Digestion is over, and the new fat begins its journey through the lymphatics to its cellular destination. Here its most important metabolic function, oxidation — burning up— will take place.[18]

A large proportion of the fat travelling along the lymphatics eventually arrives at the liver where it is met by that previously discussed lipotropic family — choline, betaine, and methionine — which engage the fat in the transfer of that special energy, the methyl group, transmethylation. In this operation, once the fats unite with phosphorus to form the phospholipids, the liver quickly moves them out and into the plasm of the blood stream where with a few of those arms still left free, the phospholipids can latch on to a lipoprotein[19] — a fat carrying protein in the plasma — to catch a final ride to their destination.

By way of our summary-at-a-glance, let's chart the digestion of fats:

1. Fats and oils in our food are taken into the mouth as three parts fatty acid, and one part glycerine. No actual molecular breakdown occurs here.

2. In the stomach, fats and oils are mixed with proteins and carbohydrates in a mass called chyme.

3. The chyme passes into the small intestine where the fat is emulsified by the bile from the liver and the gall bladder.

4. This prepares the fats for the action of steapsin, an enzyme secreted by the pancreas into the small intestine. Steapsin separates the fatty acids from the glycerine so they can mix with the alkalies of the intestinal juices. Glycerine, meanwhile, is absorbed into the lymphatics where it is rejoined shortly by the fatty acids. Thus reunited in the lymphatics, glycerine and the fatty acids now form new body fat, most of which is delivered to the liver.

5. In the liver, the lipotropic family— choline, methionine, and betaine — prepare the body fat for transport to the cells by shifting a special combination of carbon and hydrogen called the methyl group in such a way that phosphorus can combine with the fats to form phospholipids. This process called transmethylation must occur regularly or fatty deposits will develop in the liver. Once the shifting of methyl groups occurs, phospholipids proceed to the cells for oxidation.

FIG. 10: Summary of the Digestion of Fat: How the Body Releases Fatty Acid from the Fats in Food.

THE SECOND STAGE: BURNING IT UP

The next cycle, the production of energy in the cell, is the primary reason for consuming fats. Yet by our chart summary, you see how much that original food fat has to go through just to get to this point. Just as each of the enzyme co-workers helping to transform the fats into easily transported products is indispensable, and frustrations along the way can cause problematic digestion and elimination, so in this final metabolic cycle each of the intermediate products which occurs during the oxidation process *must* be converted into the next by-product which, in turn, must be converted into the next, and so on. If the chain reaction stops anywhere along the line, a build-up of one or more by-products will occur. This is a violation of nature's insistent drive to complete all her cycles. The penalty for any violation is congestion followed by the spread of toxins throughout the body. Cells weaken, become vulnerable to infectious bacteria, break down, and finally disease prevails. Preventing this from happening is what good health is all about, but it requires sufficient knowledge about how the body serves nature and takes care of itself so that we can cooperate in its work. We want to stress that quite often it is a breakdown somewhere in the oxidation cycle that causes many people needless physical suffering. Making energy out of the fats in the cells (oxidation) can either be invigorating if it functions without a hitch, or it can be debilitating if breakdowns occur. *The key to successful oxidation is knowing what micronutrients, either in the food we eat or in the food supplements we take at meals, work with the enzymes to keep the ball rolling* in this last adventure of the metabolic journey.

— LAST LAP —

As we look into this phase, the importance of eating protein is confirmed. You will recall that the amino acids are liberated from protein. They become the mother substances for enzymes, not just enzymes such as steapsin which is easily identified in the digestive process, but hundreds of enzymes and groups of less commonly identifiable enzymes that are actually microscopic forms of body protein working to transform fats into energy. As long as we continue to eat sufficient protein daily (½ gram per body pound) the critical supply should not diminish. What we need to stress here, of course, in making such a generalized statement, is that bio-chemical individuality is always the determining factor. The amount of protein we recommend is only a guideline. There are hundreds of biochemical influences exerting pressure on us at all times. Such influences may well include the co-enzymes, the non-protein elements which the body's enzymes absolutely cannot do without if they are to perform their oxidative tasks. *All co-enzymes must be taken into our bodies via food or food supplements because our bodies cannot make them out of amino acids or any other chemical substance in the cells.* The name given to these co-enzymes is *vitamins.*

Once in the cells, the first co-enzymes the fatty acids meet are their old B vitamin companions, choline and inositol. Yet even without the burning action of choline and inositol, *dehydrogenase,* an enzyme (-ase) which literally takes away hydrogen from fat *(de-hydrogen-)* by burning it up, calls upon two B vitamins, Thiamin (B1) and Niacin (B3), to co-oxidize the hydrogen. The remaining carbon particles then break up into double fragments.

At this point, fat metabolism swings into the tail end of the carbohydrate metabolic cycle. Remember?

Where the asterisk is, we discover that the double carbon fragments which make up the foundation of Acetyl CoEnzyme A are actually the carbon particles that resulted from the work of the dehydrogenases on the fatty acids.[21] What's left from these reductions serves as a groundwork for pantothenic acid, B1 and B6 to build themselves into co-enzyme A. As the metabolism continues then we see how Acetylco-enzyme A stands at the crossroads of fat and carbohydrate metabolism. See diagram p. 96.

— A SPECIAL SPOTLIGHT
FOR A SPECIAL HERO —

As a final note here, we must not neglect the anti-oxidant vitamin, Vitamin E. Vitamin E has a sparing action on the factors precipitating fat rancidity in the body. Peroxides rapidly turn fats rancid and hasten the accumulation of solid fatty particles in the bloodstream. They can be broken down with an ample supply of Vitamin E which removes the oxygen and carries it off to feed other cells. The peroxides are thereby reduced to water which passes to the kidneys and then to the bladder for excretion.

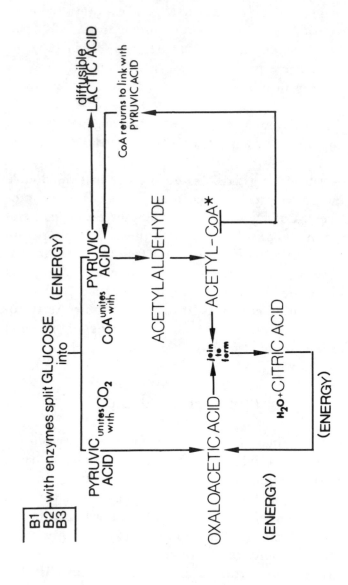

FIG.11:   Review of Citric Acid Cycle Diagrammatic.

We should caution, the more polyunsaturated fats
eaten, the more Vitamin E should be introduced into
the diet in order to protect the fats from rancidity. [22]
The antioxidant properties of Vitamin E are en-
hanced by other antioxidants such as ascorbic
acid. [23,24].

Please remember, our summaries of metabolic
processes are highly condensed versions of operations
which otherwise provide enough detailed information
about enzymatic activity to fill an entire volume. And
as biochemical research continues, many more
volumes are likely to ensue. What we intend to do by
our summaries of fat and carbohydrate metabolism is
to give you some idea of the problem areas and the
importance of vitamins as insurance for metabolic
efficiency.

— THE MOST DANGEROUS MEAL
IN THE WEST —

We come now to the dinner menus. Dinner is the
meal in which many of us tend to overindulge. There
are many contributing factors to this. First, custom
has established the dinner hour as the hour of the
daily family reunion. There is a kind of release from
the day's tensions which the family likes to celebrate
together. The leisure which surrounds the dinner hour
also contributes to overindulgence— that extra bit of
potato with sour cream, that additional hot roll with
butter. And who can refuse the wife or mother who is
such an expert at making dessert? It's so good, and
the family may just linger for a second helping.
Dinner is also the meal which many adults begin with

a cocktail— or two, or even three— which means extra calories, and they often conclude with a brandy or their favorite liqueur with coffee. This is especially true when it comes to eating in restaurants. The restaurant atmosphere is especially conducive to overindulging in high calorie foods. There are not many of us who can resist that mixed drink while waiting for our salad, and once the salad has arrived, punctuate each mouthful with a piece of tasty buttered roll or breadstick. And then, there's the dinner wine to choose, and perhaps cheeses to select, and so, on it goes.

Of course, we don't eat this way every night, and it is not what we eat occasionally that seriously unbalances the system, but rather what we eat regularly. If you are in a position, however, in which you must entertain a great deal, and especially if you must eat with colleagues or clients in restaurants infamous for their unbalanced or downright bad nutrition, be careful. Watch particularly the ease with which you pick up that second or third breadstick, casually order the second martini, or finish up a third glass of dinner wine after the meal. These unthinking acts carried on during and adding to pleasant conversation with friends, are crimes against carbohydrate and fat metabolism. Eating this way, even once a week, will eventually take its toll on the system, for overloading ourselves with carbohydrates whether they are in the form of bread, liquor, or candy and cake is one of the chief ways we have manufactured malnutrition in this country. Excessive carbohydrates dampen our appetites for other needed nutrients, particularly amino acids from protein, and place a demand on the body's supply of enzymes which cannot be replaced if the necessary amino acids which compose them are missing. Even if we do manage to eat sufficient protein, which is doubtful, once we begin to glut ourselves with carbohydrates, we rarely consume enough of the co-enzymes in the form of vitamins to complete enzymatic functions. The result, of course, is a breakdown in the chain of metabolic conversions which we have already analysed. Congestion follows; then, toxicity; all compounded by our ignorant refusal simply to give the body a rest and to supply it with the micronutrients it requires to unload the liver, the pancreas, and the colon of their cumbersome burdens.

We should therefore consider that obesity originating from this cause is a form of malnutrition. Be aware, it happens regardless of age. Mothers should know that although a nutritional balance for infants and pre-teens does require more carbohydrates than protein, the wrong kinds of carbohydrates consumed either in large portions, or too frequently, will cause more fat cells to develop into depots where the excess carbohydrates can be stored as fat. Throughout the child's life, then, these depots will constantly make demands on the body to be filled, thus contributing to the agonizing problem of obesity. The abundance of fat cells formed early in childhood by overindulgent feeding is not easily dealt with through adolescence and adulthood. Of what comfort is it to a teenager or an adult who it seems puts on weight simply by thinking about desserts, to say, "You see, I was overfed as an infant."

With this in mind, the following dinner menus are balanced so that all the cells in the body get the nutrition they need with the proper kinds of carbohydrates balanced with the necessary oils and proteins. If these menus and the ones preceding them are followed faithfully, they will obviate the need for snacks between meals. The reason is that the cells have the proper macronutrients — protein, oils, carbohydrates — and the proper micronutrients — vitamins, minerals, and enzymes— to maintain life and generate heat and energy. As to whether you should eat lightly or heavily, let natural hunger determine the amount of food you eat. If you follow the protein-oil-carbohydrate priority, your hunger will be satisfied when you have eaten what you should. At this point, stop eating, for each additional mouthful puts an extra load on the digestive and metabolic system.

We are still emphasizing vegetables and fruit as the principal carbohydrate sources for dinner. We advise keeping bread and grains down to a minimum. Ordinarily there is not enough physical activity or exercise following dinner to work off the caloric intake of these foods. If habit and custom prevail, however, one slice or one piece of whole grain bread (never white) or toast may be eaten. A good rule to follow to maintain normal weight: eat bread at lunch or at dinner, but not at both meals. And if you can do without bread altogether, do so.

The following vegetables may be either steamed or prepared in a pressure cooker to maintain their nutrition. Remember, high temperatures destroy enzymes, so the closer the vegetable remains to its raw state, the better chance you have of assimilating its maximum nutritive value.

STEAMED OR PRESSURE COOKED VEGETABLES, PREFERABLY FRESH:

potatoes

carrots

string beans

summer squash

yellow squash

zucchini

mustard greens

turnip greens

turnips

kale

collards

peas (fresh or frozen)

cauliflower

lima beans (fresh or frozen)

broccoli

brussell sprouts

cabbage

beets

asparagus

corn (fresh or frozen)

Each menu will specify either one or two steamed vegetables or a fresh vegetable salad. The fresh vegetable salad is the ideal, but its use should be governed by our ability to handle that toughest of all the polysaccharides, cellulose. If we are willing to chew thoroughly those vegetables which contain this type of sugar— and so many in their raw state do contain at least a small amount— then we are probably well prepared to consume a raw salad abundant with a variety of vegetables once or twice a day. If, however, we are not thorough chewers, or if we have problems with cellulose binding us up no matter how well we chew it, then it would be wise to add one or more glasses of fresh vegetable juice to our daily diet and to restrict ourselves to eating steamed or pressure cooked vegetables— cooked, that is, just long enough (one to ten minutes) to break down the cellulose so that it can be consumed without difficulty.

SALAD #3: THE RAW VEGETABLE SALAD
(cf. LUNCH MENUS for Salads #1 & #2)

(not necessarily consisting of *all*, but as many of the following vegetables as you may desire:)

carrots
string beans
broccoli
tomatoes
turnips
radishes
cucumbers
black olives
green peppers
endive
romaine lettuce
alfalfa sprouts.

THE BALANCED SUPPER

MENU 1.
> *3 ½ oz. whole meat: steak, beef, lamb, broiled or oven baked, with*
> *A: baked potato; one steamed vegetable; salad #1 with polyunsaturated oil dressing.*
> *B: two steamed vegetables; salad #1 or #2 with polyunsaturated oil dressing.*
> *C: salad #3 with polyunsaturated oil dressing.*

COMMENT:

Regarding 1-A, if a baked potato was eaten at lunch, choose either 1-B or 1-C. The baked potato is a wholesome food, consisting of good carbohydrate and high quality protein, and should be eaten from once to three times weekly, but not twice in one day.

Do not omit the oil dressing. It should include a Tbsp. of polyunsaturated oil. If you choose to use lemon juice on your salad, either dress your vegetables with polyunsaturated oil mayonnaise, or supplement your meal with polyunsaturated oil capsules. Recall that our emphasis here is justified on the basis of the necessity of oils in the diet. You will more than likely get that hunger pang before bedtime if you don't include them.

If you are one of those people adversely affected with gas after combining starch and meat, omit 1-A altogether from your diet. For some people, sugar and protein ingested together cause more rapid putrefaction in the intestine. Better for you to choose 1-B or 1-C.

NOTE: For a delicious sweetener to accompany your lamb try fresh chopped pineapple combined with fresh chopped mint leaves.

MENU 2.
3½ oz. baked or broiled fish with A: wild or whole grain rice; one steamed vegetable; salad #1 with polyunsaturated oil dressing.
B: two steamed vegetables; salad #1 or #2 with polyunsaturated oil dressing.
C: salad #3 with polyunsaturated oil dressing.

COMMENT:
A word of advice on serving your carbohydrates. Saturated fat retards the digestion of starch, so it would be well not to saturate your potato or rice with butter. It's hard enough to get into the habit of mixing such foods well with the saliva in the mouth before swallowing without making it harder for the digestive system by retarding enzymatic activity with excess fat.

Here's a suggestion for preparing the fish. Using sole, flounder, perch or haddock, bread the pieces in soy flour or in a combination of soy flour and wheat germ, preferably defatted wheat germ. This will boost the protein content of the fish and give it greater body as well. If you choose to fry the fish, use a Teflon pan or a small amount of butter, as we suggested in the breakfast menu. Fry lightly over moderate heat for only one or two minutes. On the platter, the fish may be garnished with slices of hard boiled egg, steamed mushrooms, slivered almonds and lemon slices.

Here is one of our favorite rice recipes: Place one cup of uncooked rice and two cups of cold water in a pot ready for boiling. Add 1 Tbsp. Oregano, ½ cup presoaked raisins, ½ cup sliced mushrooms, ¼ tsp. onion powder, ¼ tsp. garlic powder. Bring to a boil, then simmer for approximately forty minutes, or until rice is tender. Add polyunsaturated oil or butter before serving. Makes 3-4 servings.

MENU 3.

3½ oz. of chicken or turkey with
A: baked yam & honey; steamed
vegetable; salad #1 or #2 with
polyunsaturated oil dressing.
B: two steamed vegetables; salad
#1 or #2 with polyunsaturated
oil dressing.
C: salad #3 with polyun-
saturated oil dressing.

COMMENT:

Rice or potato, of course, may be substituted for the yam, if desired. If a dressing composed of bread or nuts is served with the poultry dinner, it is advisable to omit the yam, rice or potato. Menu 3B or

3C provides more than ample carbohydrate nutrition.

Many people follow the custom of serving cran-
berry sauce with a turkey dinner. If this is done, it is
advisable at some other meal to choose foods rich in
calcium, or take a calcium supplement. The reason
for this is that cranberries, as well as spinach and
rhubarb and chard, contain *oxalic acid* which unites
with the calcium in the food and forms an insoluble
salt, *calcium oxalate*, which passes right through the
body. Thus, to a large degree, the calcium contained
in such foods is not made available to our bodies.

NOTE: Do not cook the yam *with honey*, rather add
the honey afterwards.

> MENU 4.
> *3½ oz. serving of beef or calf liver*
> *with*
> *A: baked yam & honey; steamed*
> *vegetable; salad #1 or #2 with*
> *polyunsaturated oil dressing.*
> *B: two steamed vegetables; salad*
> *#1 or #2 with polyunsaturated*
> *oil dressing.*
> *C: salad #3 with polyun-*
> *saturated oil dressing.*

COMMENT:
Since liver is one of the most wholesome foods we
can eat, include it in the diet at least once weekly.
Due to the presence of choline and methionine which
are engaged in the transmethylation process, this
organ meat is rich in polyunsaturates and emulsifying

factors, moreso than any other meat. If liver is too unappealing, it is advisable to take the food in capsule or tablet form daily.

As a variation of the liver menu, we recommend the gland-organ protein drink. This consists of 2 Tbsp. of a gland-organ protein powder (dessicated beef liver, pancreas, spleen, duodenum, heart) or simply a Tbsp. of a liver powder, dessicated and defatted, mixed thoroughly in an 8 oz. glass of tomato juice. Thus:

THE SUPPER DRINKS

MENU 5:

> *Liver protein Drink; Salad #3 with polyunsaturated oil dressing*

COMMENT:

This may appear to be a light supper, but the hefty protein drink (18-20 grams of protein) is filling, while the vegetables in the salad supply abundant carbohydrate nutrition and the oil in the dressing supplies the needed fats. It may also be substituted as a lunch drink, if desired.

MENU 6.

> *Natural food protein drink; Salad #3 with polyunsaturated oil dressing.*

COMMENT:

This second suggestion for a supper drink is based on the following recipe:

1 Tbsp. Natural Food Protein Powder.

½ cup milk, non-fat, low-fat, or whole milk.

½ cup fruit juice (your choice).

1 Tbsp. skim milk powder.

1 raw fertile egg.

1 Tbsp. wheat germ oil or almond oil.

Mix the ingredients well in a blender.

Serve in a chilled glass, with salad.

MENU 7.

This is a low stress diet designed by biochemist Stuart Wheelwright, Ph.D, of Life Centers, Inc. Ogden, Utah, for those who wish to correct the pH balance of the blood. As reflected in the urine by daily testing with a LoBuff tape for 20 days *at each urination*, the pH reading will, if charted, reveal two acid cycles and two alkaline cycles. The following acidifying menu plan eaten twice daily is capable of keeping the acid-alkaline balance under control so that an ideal pH reading between 5.5 and 6 is maintained during the active hours of the day. A pH so maintained supports the body under the usual stresses which otherwise weaken resistance to disease.

8 A.M. BREAKFAST:

Fruit. Exclude citrus. (If melon is eaten, exclude all other fruits. Other fruits may be combined in a salad.)

11 A.M. and 4 or 5 P.M. Lunch and Dinner:

(1) 3-4 oz. fish with 1 tsp. of cottage cheese

(2) A small salad consisting of alfalfa or lentil sprouts with 1 tsp. of mixed seeds including any or all of the following: sunflower seeds, pumpkin seeds, sesame seeds, chia seeds, flax or psyllium seeds. Combine with homemade dressing composed of sesame oil and apple cider vinegar with herbal seasonings of your own choice.

(3) Five mixed steamed vegetables selected from the follow-

ing: broccoli, zucchini, cauliflower, string beans, carrots, turnips, parsnips, beets, Jerusalem artichokes. Exclude all starches in the form of bread, rice and potatoes in this diet. A fresh vegetable salad may be substituted for the steamed vegetables at ONE of the meals; thus, the small salad above in (2) may be combined with any of the following raw vegetables in a larger salad: lettuce (choose butter or romaine, but exclude head lettuce), cucumbers, radishes, carrots, celery, avocado (¼ only), watercress, zucchini, broccoli, cauliflower.

(4) Finally, include 1 cup of hydrolized amino acid broth by placing two tsp. of amino acid compound powder in 1 cup hot water. Or, as an alternative, include five hydrolized protein wafers at the meal.

This meal is called the **FIVE AND FIVE** because it consists of **A)** five protein sources providing a broad spectrum of amino acid coverage and **B)** five vegetables providing high quality non-starch carbohydrate. Remember, the oil is of major importance in the meal and must never be omitted. Along with the vegetables, it serves as a necessary buffer for the proteins. Thus we have a balance of all three essential nutrients.

THE COLD SUPPER

MENU 8.

> *Swiss or any white cheese; Raw tomato with diced green onion; Polyunsaturated oil dressing with*
> *A: Egg Salad.*
> *B: Chicken salad.*
> *C: Tuna, salmon, or shrimp salad.*

MENU 9.

> *The Waldorf Salad, with a protein drink from Menu 5 or 6.*

COMMENT:

The waldorf salad is delicious and contains a

complete protein balanced with carbohydrates and fatty acid nutrition. Alone, however, it may not satisfy, simply because it may not be enough food. But as a light supper snack when you aren't too hungry, it's perfect.

Recipe:

Ingredients: apples, walnuts, raisins, celery, polyun-saturated oil mayonnaise, lemon juice.

Dice one or two apples and soak in lemon juice or add immediately to the mayonnaise in order to prevent darkening of the fruit from exposure to the air. Chop ¼ lb. walnuts (or as many as desired) and add to the apples. Add ½ cup of presoaked raisins, and mix thoroughly with ½ cup or more of polyun-saturated oil mayonnaise. Serve chilled. Truly yummy.

MENU 10.
> *One whole apple, sliced, soaked in lemon juice.*
> *¼ lb. almonds.*
> *2 or 3 sticks of celery.*
> *Protein drink from Menu 5 or 6.*

COMMENT:
    Here's another delightful light supper that supplies balanced nutrition. The apple-almond-celery combination makes an excellent snack any time the need for nutrition is felt. Like the waldorf salad, it is a perfect balance of protein, oils, and carbohydrates.

MENU 11.

Steamed lima beans sprinkled with nutseed meal.

Top with one scoop (½ cup) of cottage cheese.

Salad #1 or #2 with polyunsaturated oil dressing.

COMMENT:

This combination of limas and cottage cheese will surprise you. It is quite tasty and affords double protein value, since limas contain more protein than most vegetables.

It should be noted that the luncheon and dinner menus are, of course, interchangeable, and any one may be substituted for another.

The question of dessert is inevitable, so we have designed a number of dessert possibilities based on fruit combinations that we think are delicious and satisfying. They are strictly carbohydrate nutrition. If the fruit combinations are used as desserts (dried fruits excepted) eat them approximately one hour after the close of the meal.

FRUIT COMBINATIONS FOR
DESSERTS OR SNACKS:

1.

¼ or ½ melon with center scooped out.
3/4 to one cup seedless green grapes in center.

2.

¼ or ½ melon with center scooped out.
3/4 to one cup of diced strawberries in center.

3.

1 large banana sliced lengthwise.
garnished with 3/4 cup seedless green grapes.

4.

1/3 cup of each:
diced watermelon.
diced pineapple.
diced papaya.
seedless green grapes.
Mix well in juices of the fruit. Chill.

5.

Sliced pears, one medium size, ripe, in eighths.
Walnut halves dipped in honey, ½ cup.
¼ cup diced white cheese.
½ cup seedless green grapes.

6.

Baked Apple Supreme:

Bake one medium sized golden delicious apple in 500° oven until soft. Remove and top with presoaked raisins, about ¼ cup.

Coat with honey and sprinkle with cinnamon and 1 tsp. of nutseed meal.

NOTE: Just about any fruit outside of citrus is delicious with the nutseed meal sprinkled on it.

FAT REVIEW

TIPS THAT MAKE A DIFFERENCE:

1. Allowing for biochemical individuality, the basic polyunsaturated oil requirement is approximately 2-3 Tbsp. daily, so that the body may get its supply of linoleic acid.
2. At any meal, always balance saturated fats with raw polyunsaturated oils (at least 2:1) and emulsify them with lecithin.
3. Remember, any polyunsaturated oil becomes hydrogenated and thus saturated when it is heated.
4. Keep the transmethylation pathways open in the liver with supplements of choline, inositol, betaine and amino acid broth which contains methionine.

The metabolism and oxidation of fats brings us to the end of the body's utilization of the macro-nutrients. A thorough coverage, however, should include a consideration of the manner in which the waste products of protein, fat, and carbohydrate digestion are eliminated. This is a subject too often glossed over, even ignored by many nutritionists. For reasons which we shall discover, this is not a wise omission.

CHAPTER FIVE:

AN UNGLAMOROUS SUBJECT —

Verily, but we hasten to repeat, a necessary one. Practicing efficient elimination is as fundamental to good health as practicing balanced nutrition. Yet understanding and caring for the organs of excretion to help the body to adequately eliminate the wastes of macronutrient metabolism are neglected by many people. Of the four main organs of elimination — the sweat glands, the tear ducts, the kidneys and the colon, there is little to say about the first two, and the nature of the kidneys will be discussed in the last chapter. This leaves the colon which is responsible for handling all of the body's solid waste material.

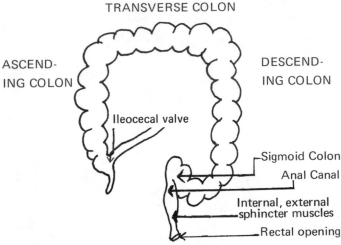

FIG. 12: The Colon.

In explaining the elimination of solid waste, we should start by explaining just what is meant by a bowel movement. The fecal or waste material which accumulates in the bowel or sigmoid colon (see diagram) must be pushed out through the anal canal. But this passage is controlled by the contraction and relaxation of the sphincter muscles. When the fecal material builds up in the *sigmoid* colon, impulses from that area shoot up the spine along the afferent nerve, and then downward along the efferent nerve, setting into spiral motion three valves in the sigmoid colon. The spiral movement of the valves forces the fecal matter out resulting in what we commonly refer to as a bowel movement. [1]

The "bowel movement," however, is merely the last phase of a continual movement that starts when the partially digested chyme passes from the stomach through the pyloric valve into the small intestine. A constant snake-like movement called *peristalsis* keeps the chyme moving through the small intestine until all the digested nutrients are absorbed through the villi along the inside of the intestinal wall. The waste products which remain then pass from the ileum (the lowest part of the small intestine) into the cecum (the lowest part of the ascending colon) through the *ileocecal* valve.[2] This valve normally opens only into the colon.[3] If due to congestion in the colon the fecal matter from there backs up, forcing the ileocecal valve to open in the opposite direction as waste matter reenters the ileum, nausea occurs and very often vomiting. More often than not, this is really the upset stomach we experience. It is not the stomach at all. It is the kickback from a congested intestinal tract as it tries to acquire some breathing space. If due to moderate eating and balanced nutrition, the colon is in good condition, the fecal matter moves along, and good evacuations will occur two to three times within twenty-four hours. It is only when fecal matter remains in the colon between thirty-three to seventy-two hours that it causes gas, putrefaction, and an unsuitable alkaline medium.

Congestion is one of the most serious problems confronting intestinal health. It occurs most frequently in the corners where the transverse colon connects the ascending and descending colons. Pockets of fecal matter may accumulate in these corners, eventually obstructing the passageway much in the same manner as accumulated fatty deposits on the walls of the arteries obstruct the flow of blood. If congestion continues, layer after layer of waste hardens and accumulates on the colon walls until there is only a tiny space left for waste material to pass through.

This is evident when stool is stringy, scarce, and about the diameter of a lead pencil. After seventy-two hours, the healthy acid environment of the colon turns alkaline. This alkaline medium gives the strep bacteria a chance to thrive, which kills the protective friendly bacilli in the mucosal cells. The mucous sloughs off — much can be detected in the stool — permitting the toxins to pass through the often spastic, over-stretched epithelial cells of the intestinal wall into the blood stream.[4] In our experience we have found that this is not a rare occurrence. It is all too common. It is the beginning of pathology. Unfortunately, there is still controversy about whether toxins do, in fact, enter the blood stream by way of the colon wall. Specifically, toxins travel by way of the blood vessels connecting the colon and the small intestine and the liver. Thus, as toxins back up in these blood vessels, the liver becomes congested, and in order to free itself to perform its critical functions, it throws off these toxins into the circulatory system. But if toxins can pass through, nutrients following the same law of mass action can pass through just as readily. We have witnessed cases in which it was impossible to feed patients orally. They were successfully both fed and medicated through the rectum. In one particular case which we recall, B12 was injected rectally into a patient. Before the syringe was emptied, the patient had the distinct taste of B12 in his mouth.

Tracing colon-released toxins such as guanadine and histamine in the blood stream reveal how these poisons can accumulate in the cells. The toxins pass from the colon to the liver, as we said, and eventually the impaired liver gets so congested from having to

work overtime that it must throw more and more of
the toxins back into the blood stream as the red
blood cells move on to the lungs to receive oxygen.[5]
However, the blood by this time is toxic enough that
the cells are unable to absorb enough oxygen to
recycle the lactic acid from the muscle cells. This is
why sore and aching muscles often accompany the
signs of colon congestion. The toxicity in the blood
stream, especially guanadine, likewise interferes with
capillary supply around the joints so that bursitis and
arthritis may be aggravated. In our experience it is
rare that an arthritic victim does not also have
problems with constipation. The entrance of such a
blood supply into the nervous system irritates the
nerves, precipitating neuritis, and since the vagus
nerve is especially irritated, headaches of varying
intensities periodically occur.

The kidneys, whose function it is to purify the
blood stream, cannot completely filter the heavy
toxins out of the blood, and as a result they remain in
the bloodstream and circulate to the cells where
gradually they so interfere with metabolism that
often the cells cannot properly oxidize the nutrients,
or if they are able to oxidize, the waste products get
trapped with the toxins. This additional congestion
causes the membranes of the cell walls to tear, and
cells decompose more rapidly sending additional
waste products into the bloodstream and thence to
the kidneys where, combined with uric acid crystals,
they may do additional damage by tearing the
membranes of the filtering mechanisms.

After a time the combination of poorly toned

stomach muscles and the weight of the transverse colon filled with fecal matter brings about a pronounced droop, a *prolapsis,* in the transverse colon. An additional cause may precipitate a prolapsed colon. The stomach also has begun to droop, forming what medical men call a "fish hook" stomach.

The fish hook causes many unpleasant digestive problems. In our experience one of the most common is a growing inability to pass oils from the stomach through the pyloric valve into the small intestine. They remain in the stomach so long that nausea and vomiting ensue. Sufferers have no choice but to eliminate oils from their diet which weakens their energy, taxes cell membranes and dries up the skin.

The colon, meanwhile, attempting to perform its regular movements, struggles under the prolapsed condition and the build-up of hardened fecal matter. It stretches, elongates, and develops spasms (spastic colitis), so that in some areas the colon becomes ballooned, and in others narrowly constricted.

The foreseeable results of prolonging this condition include diverticulitis, in which fecal matter becomes imbedded in sacks along the wall of the colon; and hemorrhoids, in which the pressure of constipation frustrates the natural colon movements, irritating the muscular blood vessels so that they become varicose, i.e., knotted, swollen, and extremely painful. If constipation is not relieved, the lining of the colon becomes so irritated that the body draws out water and bile salts from the accumulated fecal matter and expels them through the anal passage, an occurrence we experience as diarrhea. Although in these cases some fecal matter may accompany the water and bile fluid, much of the fecal matter remains behind in the congested areas of the colon. Since "the runs" expel much less fecal matter than we assume, diarrhea actually calls for a thorough sometimes professional cleansing of the large intestine.

All of this paints a pretty bleak picture. However, good colon health is possible without extreme measures except in extreme cases of constipation, diverticulitis, spastic colitis, mucous colitis, etc., which require medical attention. Good colon health starts in the same place digestion starts— in the mouth. *Thorough mastication of all our food is essential.* Food should be chewed until it is mush. If we do not take this first step consistently, we have no one to blame for intestinal disorders except ourselves. Most of us are lazy chewers, and we swallow our food long before we should. After only ten chomps or so, the epiglotus in the rear of the mouth dilates automatically and allows food to drop prematurely into the esophagus, as a reflex from years of improper eating habits.

Improperly chewed food makes the gastric juices work harder. The stomach churns the mixture of gastric enzymes and masticated food into chyme. If the stomach cannot complete its digestive operations due to improper chewing or diluted hydrochloric acid and pepsin, which, incidentally, is quite common,[6] the food must pass through the pyloric valve only partially digested. The first two rules, then, for maintaining colon health are: *first, chew solid food until it has the consistency of mush, which in some cases may require chewing between thirty to fifty times; second, be sure to replenish the gastric enzymes, HCL and pepsin, if their deficiency is indicated either by insufficient protein digestion or by a medical examination.*

The liver and the pancreas are the two glands whose digestive secretions complete the breakdown of food energy into body energy. The liver secretes bile for the digestion of fats, while the pancreas stimulates the manufacture of hydrochloric acid in the stomach, secretes trypsin for the digestion of protein, steapsin for the digestion of fats, and amylopsin for the digestion of starch. If these organs are weakened by congestion, they will not function properly. *Even if there has not been any overeating, we should all take one day during the week and restrict our nutritional intake to apple juice and water which will give these organs a rest.* Apple juice will keep the blood sugar up so the energy level does not drop and hunger pangs are avoided. It will also help restore an acid condition to the colon if an alkaline medium is imminent due to putrefaction. Bile salts and pancreatin may be taken orally to stimulate these organs to regain their natural vigor. The liver, if congested, may also be relieved by drinking a tea made from beet tops.

— RECIPE FOR BEET LEAF TEA —

Place beet tops in a pot. Add eight cups of water. Bring to a boil. Turn off heat and let remain. Drink a total of six cups of this tea throughout the day, preferably alternating with the apple juice and water on the day of a fast.

The pancreas is additionally important to colon health since it secretes a solution which lubricates the fecal matter in the colon. Thus the third rule is to take care of the liver and the pancreas by eating meals properly balanced with all essential nutrients so that neither organ is overtaxed to supply any necessary enzyme. The weekly day of fasting is recommended to give the organs a chance to restore themselves if they have been overtaxed.

Along with a balanced diet, one tablespoon of black cherry concentrate mixed with one ounce of chlorophyll in an 8 oz. glass of water taken daily is one of the most refreshing ways to keep the liver detoxified and functioning properly.

A fourth rule to follow is to avoid any food which in any one individual's case irritates the colon. The sensitivity of the mucosal lining differs in each of us so that roughage which one person can easily tolerate may create irritation in another. We must each learn this from our own experience with food.

A fifth rule is to work with the rhythms which

nature establishes in our bodies. Unfettered by disease, digestion and metabolism establish and follow their specific rhythms. Elimination will naturally do the same. Just as we should eat at the same time every day, we should also eliminate waste at regular intervals to aid and abet the nutritional cycles. Rhythmic eating balanced with rhythmic elimination protects the cells against destructive congestion and, all else being equal, assures us that maximum nutrition is getting to all the tissues and organs of the body. If our elimination rhythm is off, we should re-establish it, first by assigning ourselves specific times to eat each of our three nutritionally balanced meals of the day, and *we should not deviate from this schedule.* Next, we should assign ourselves two specific times during the day to have a bowel movement. This is exactly what it appears to be: potty retraining. It takes patience and determination for an adult to retrain himself by sitting on a commode and waiting ten or fifteen minutes twice a day with perhaps little results at first; yet perseverence will ultimately re-establish a rhythm, and such a simple matter as rhythmic elimination will improve our nutritional health.

As a sixth rule, it is advisable to include certain foods in our diet which facilitate efficient evacuation. Foremost is the acidophilus bacillus found in buttermilk, yogurt, and various food supplements. This friendly bacteria which should remain implanted in the intestine retains the acid medium necessary for proper and thorough elimination. A little vinegar or lemon juice in warm water is also good to take each day for maintaining the acid medium. For additional flavor and sustained efficiency in the liver and colon, add a Tbsp. of the black cherry concentrate or apple concentrate to the yogurt. Foods containing cellulose or bran are important for increasing the transit time of waste passing through the colon.[7] We have already cautioned against the danger of too much cellulose; and too much bran, flaxseed, or similar foods which swell in the colon if not accompanied by a vigorous exercise program (see rule #7) will not accomplish what is intended. Other foods and herbs help either to keep the colon relaxed and free from spasms or to help soften fecal matter which may become hardened if the body should need to draw water from the colon. Whey, especially delicious sprinkled on fruit, for example, coats the colon wall to protect against irritation while natural chlorophyll soothes any irritated portions and kills guanadine on contact. Natural herbs, such as foenugreek, valerian root, mandrake root, and hops, help to relax the colon and are available either as teas or in tablet form. Other herbs such as culver, barberry, and aloes help to keep fecal matter soft by drawing water back into the colon.

Exercise is the seventh rule. A regular regime should be established whereby the lungs, the heart, and all the muscles of the body are systematically exercised for proper aeration of the blood, an increase of circulation, and the release of lactic acid from the muscles. Stomach muscles should be toned daily to avoid a prolapsis of the transverse colon.

An eighth rule to follow is to avoid laxatives and enemas as much as possible. A laxative other than that of a bulk nature (see below), and unless it is composed of herbs which draw water into the colon, does little to tone the colon or renew peristaltic action, and often contains chemicals which irritate the mucosal lining and interfere with muscular reactions in the colon. Enemas, which are rarely administered properly, tend to balloon the anal canal and the sigmoid colon. Figure No. 15, p. 128 for example, shows an X-Ray photograph of a patient who took frequent and poorly administered enemas.

Nonetheless, if special treatments are required to restore health to the colon, they should not be neglected. Among current therapies, three seem to be most sensible. First, *sine wave treatments,* in which electrode pads are placed on the outside of the body over the abdominal muscles which support the colon. The generated impulses pull up the weakened abdominal muscles, restore the blood circulation, and adjust the chemistry of the muscle so the lactic acid can be recycled.(cf.Figures 16-17 p. 129-30). Second, *ultra sound treatments* in which the barely perceptible heat of the ultra sound decongests the muscles and the colon. Third, *colon irrigation,* by which an efficient administration cleans out the colon with a water based solution. Even a properly administered enema will only reach the anal canal and perhaps the sigmoid colon, but a pressure controlled colon irrigation which permits no pressure in the colon wall over ¼ pound protects against ballooning, and through successive emptyings and refillings allows water to fill and wash out the entire descending and transverse colons. This method is designed to clean out the pockets of hardened fecal matter which have accumulated in the corners. It also straightens out spastic areas.(cf. Fig.18-19 p. 130-31). The solution used to wash out the colon should contain: a) water, the chief cleansing agent; b) acidophilus bacillus and vinegar to restore the acid medium and to implant the friendly bacteria culture in the mucosal cells; c) chlorophyll, to soothe intestinal lining e.g. by destroying guanadine); and d) honey, to sustain the blood sugar level which may drop and cause slight fatigue and hunger after the irrigation. (Figures No. 17 & 20 illustrate the effect of colon therapy.)

It is our opinion that under ordinary circumstances colon irrigations should not be self-administered. Anyone seeking a professionally administered colonic might do well to inquire how strictly the above requirements are followed in the treatment.

In lieu of safe and thorough colonic treatments, however, many people might choose bulk laxatives which swell in the colon and pick up some of the fecal matter which has accumulated around the walls. Such laxatives are quite useful if they are taken properly with a generous amount of fluids. Label directions, of course, should be carefully followed.

These seven rules for colon health should be followed faithfully. So many of the diseases we suffer from, if they do not originate in the large intestine, at least relate to toxic conditions resulting from poor elimination. Though serious, advanced illnesses may not be cured by colon therapy, the burden of endurance is unquestionably eased by consistent elimination of solid waste.

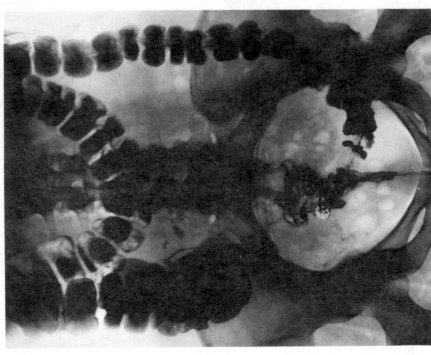

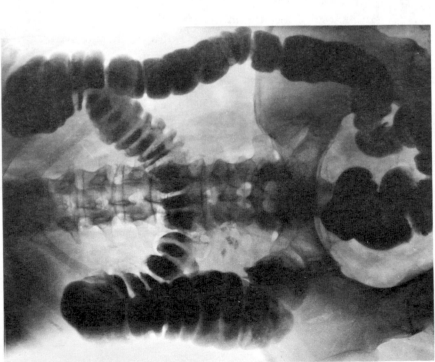

FIG. 13: A normal colon. Though there is a slight prolapse, this picture represents a colon that is as close to normal as can be observed today.

FIG. 14: The same colon demonstrating weak peristaltic action. The colon does not empty as thoroughly as it should.

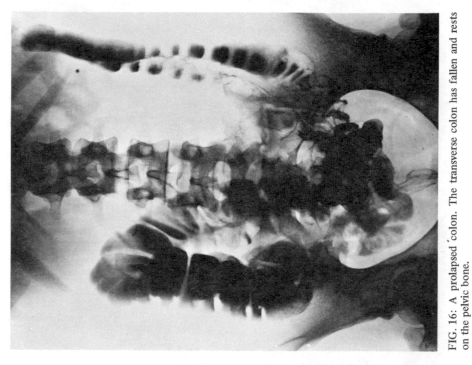

FIG. 16: A prolapsed colon. The transverse colon has fallen and rests on the pelvic bone.

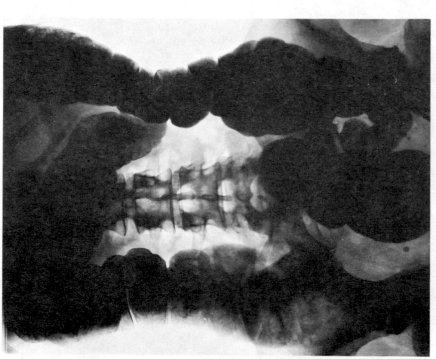

FIG. 15: A ballooned sigmoid colon, the result of too many frequent and poorly administered enemas.

TYPES OF SPASMS:

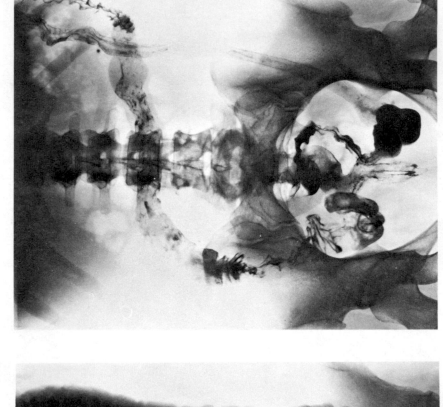

FIG. 17: (Same colon as FIG. 16) After treatment with sine waves and after exercise on the part of the patient, the transverse colon is seen

FIG. 18: A tubular spasm in the descending colon (right side of picture). Notice the narrow constriction all the way down.

TYPES OF SPASMS:

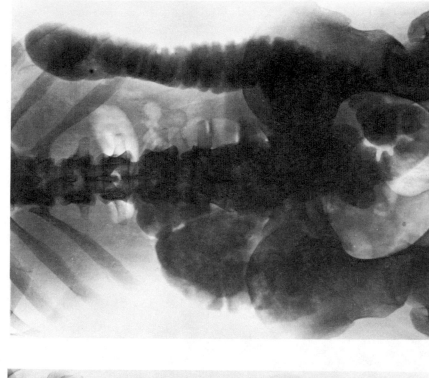

FIG. 20: Same colon as in FIG. 19 after colonic irrigation and sine wave treatment.

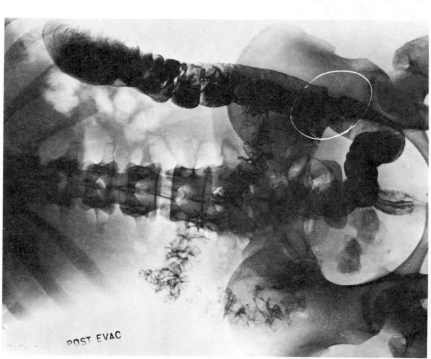

POST EVAC

FIG. 19: An anular spasm (prior to treatment) is seen in the circled constriction area of the descending colon.

To put into the digestive tract food which irritates and congests the intestine, to overeat or to eat meals so unbalanced that stress is placed on the organs responsible for secreting digestive enzymes, to neglect to masticate food, and to ignore what we wish to consider minor digestive or vague internal problems is to invite intestinal irregularities which eventually develop into otherwise avoidable pathological conditions. If we are wise enough to enjoy balanced nutrition, we should be equally wise in managing the proper disposal of its waste.

CHAPTER SIX:

VITAMINS—PROJECTS IN HARMONY

For a long time, the consumption of vitamins has centered around curative and preventative measures against certain diseases which were brought about by the lack of vitamins. Lately, scientists and laymen alike have invested more interest in the basic understanding of how these organic micronutrients work together in organized patterns to break down the tough macronutrients we consume at meals. Through the recent years of their discoveries, vitamins have earned the title of co-enzymes, a term we use to indicate how the non-proteinous vitamins work with the proteinous enzymes to convert the larger food molecules into body tissue and energy. Some of these co-enzymes are fat soluble, while others are water soluble. Though a classification such as fat soluble or water soluble suggests their mode of operation in the body, it barely suggests the vitamins' complex activity as co-enzymatic workers. Many textbooks and subsequently the popular works on vitamins treat their characteristics under these categories. However, the authors seldom give the vitamins their complete scope, and do not give the reader an organized visual scheme to plot the course of all vitamins, i.e., their co-enzymatic activity in the body.

Since we have explained the importance of eating meals balanced with sufficient protein, oils, and carbohydrates, we will explain precisely the role vitamins play in the conversion of these nutrients into energy and body tissue.

— NOT WHAT THEY CURE, BUT WHAT THEY SUSTAIN —

This is how we should always consider vitamins: not whether this one or that one will cure our backaches, allergies, or constipation, though they may alleviate such conditions, but rather whether in the food and food supplements I am taking, I have provided a sufficient vitamin balance expedient for co-enzymatic activity. *The vitamins, with few exceptions, must be considered as the fourth essential, that is, they fall under the first condition nature has set up. Like the eight essential amino acids and the essential fatty acids, they must be taken in from the outside in order to complete and sustain our interior biological functions.*

As usual, we will insist on our framework of the

protein-oil-carbohydrate priority for a foundation. In so doing, let's see how the vitamins promote harmony in building a sound body.

Helping to metabolize protein:
Vitamins C,A,K,D,and B.

Helping to metabolize oils:
Vitamins A,K,D,E,B.

Helping to metabolize carbohydrates:
Vitamin B.

As you can see, there are overlappings, yet in our practical living and building of a healthy body, this classification provides a perspective that dissipates much of the current confusion arising from misinformation about vitamins. The secret lies in hinging a vitamin's activity on its specific relationship to the body's three basic nutrients. A succinct diagram will summarize it at a glance. (See page 152).

The vitamins that service protein participate in at least four of the body's life-promoting projects. The manufacture of collagen, epithelium, fibrin, and the process of calcification. By the harmonizing work of C,A,K,D, and B, tissue, blood, and bone are stabilized and protected.

THE COLLAGEN PROJECT

Our first hero, Vitamin C or Ascorbic Acid, helps to synthesize chiefly three protein substances: collagen, thyroxin, and adrenalin. It also performs a special function with a group of detoxifiers, protein in origin, called phagocytes. Each of these special activities demonstrates ascorbic acid's remarkable versatility in the body.

Collagen is a protein fiber found throughout the body's connective tissue. It supports, protects, and cements all the bodily organs. In its ideal state it is strong enough to prevent cellular invasion by staph and strep bacteria. The tougher the collagen, the safer the body. And so, to insure this protection, Vitamin C links with the body's iron and catalyzes two amino acids, proline and lysine to form and secure the collagenous tissue. [1]

Once vitamin C finishes its synthesizing task, it is gone, which is why the cells must be bathed repeatedly in ample tides of the vitamin. When this happens, infections and disease are diverted because the body is protected by C's strong vigilance.

Yet additional sacrifice is required of C. It has long been known that as an extension of its protective power over the cells, its reputation as a detoxifier is derived from its association with an army of well-arm- ed soldiers, the phagocytes. This legion of white corpuscles— protein in origin— along with many troops of antibodies is the chief source of detoxifica- tion in the body. Like devouring sponges, the phagocytes attack and absorb microorganisms in- vading the body. This absorption is fatal to the phagocytes, however, and like ascorbic acid, the phagocytes sacrifice themselves in battle. It must be pointed out, however, that it is the activating power of ascorbic acid which makes vital storm troopers out of them. The more liberal support C gives the phagocytes, the freer the cells remain from infection.

Abundant in the connective tissue around the intestines is an amino acid, tyrosine. Tyrosine is responsible for synthesizing two of the body's most important hormones, thyroxin and adrenalin. It is also present in varying degrees in the brain, the red blood cells, the albumen and globulin in the blood serum, in pepsin, and in insulin. In the process of synthesizing adrenalin, tyrosine calls upon Vitamin C,[2] using it possibly in combination with nucleic acid as a co-enzyme component to help manufacture the adrenal hormone.[3] This accounts for substantial amounts of Vitamin C found in the adrenal glands, the only place in the body, apparently, where Vitamin C is stored in any significant quantity.[4]

You'll recall, however, that nothing in the body works alone. Each element is biologically dependent on the contribution of another element, creating a vast network of interdependent systems eventuating in what we call the metabolism of the body. In its association with tyrosine, Vitamin C also has its helpers.[5] These helpers are currently included as part of the "Vitamin C Complex" — a popular phrase, though one that is not altogether chemically accurate. It is difficult, moreover, to assess the basic bio-chemistry of the helpers, currently labeled "the Vitamin P Group" — quercitrin, hesperidin, various flavones, and special glycosides such as rutin.[6] Research in the Vitamin P group suggests that these factors make possible the action of adrenalin and nor-adrenalin, and enable the body to retain Vitamin C for a longer time. It is believed that through its influence on adrenalin and Vitamin C, the P Factors, particularly the bioflavonoids strengthen the capillaries. These peripheral("P") canals, finer than a hair, are so fragile that they constantly break and must be repaired by the body. Clinical experiments indicate that liberal doses of the P factors along with Vitamin C enable the body to rebuild and fortify these capillaries so that blood may continue to flow uninterrupted from the arterioles (the smallest arteries) to the venules (the smallest veins).

In spite of the controversy over Vitamin C, the success users have had with it is due principally to the sacrifice it makes of itself to the building power of proteins and amino acids in the body. Until we ascertain further biochemical properties of ascorbic acid, the soundness of whatever claims are made about it will depend on the biological functions just described.

— NO STANDARDIZED HUMAN PACKAGE —

The "recommended daily allowance", like the minimum daily wage, represents the subsistence level of the vitamin for your body. A daily allowance below the RDA would constitute a deficiency level in most cases. We must caution, therefore, against any quoted allowance which might suggest a standardized dosage, since there is no such thing as an average man or a standardized human package. Individual biochemical differences make standarized recommendations obsolete. In making a personal decision about dosage, take cognizance of these simple guidelines:

1) Vitamin C has a widespread versatility in the body. 2) It is an innocuous substance. 3) Individual experimentation is necessary, and in this case it is more salutary to err on the excess side of the scale than on the deficit side.

The foods most potent in Vitamin C are listed in the order of their potency in Section A in the Appendix.

THE EPITHELIUM PROJECT

The next body protein to consider is skin. Skin is not one but eleven layers of tissue.[7] The outer layer, called the epidermis, is composed of cells which have lost their nuclei, i.e., their life centers. They harden and form a protective layer over the entire body. The four layers underneath retain their nuclei and perform various functions, such as secreting mucous, and supporting connective tissue, blood vessels, lymphatics, nerves, the nerve endings and the sweat glands. The name given to these proteinous layers of tissue is epithelium.[8] *Epithelium covers any organ or part of the body which deals with the entrance of any foreign body, not only invading bacteria, but air, food, drink, and their waste products as well.* Consider then the number of organs which must be lined with protective epithelium in order to insure safe operation: the alimentary canal, the digestive organs, the organs of elimination, the sexual organs, the respiratory organs. All must be maintained by a layer of healthy epithelium.[9] Nature hands over the responsibility of maintaining the integrity of the epithelium to Vitamin A. Yet strangely enough, *the enzyme reaction process which actually accounts for Vitamin A's protective ability is still unknown. Its salutary power to maintain epithelium, however, is clinically incontestable.*

The chemical name for Vitamin A is retinol. Retinol occurs in animal foods as an ester, i.e. an organic alcohol of the animal's fatty acids. In our digestion, retinol must be treated by special pancreatic enzymes (ester-ases) which hydrolyse the vitamin so it may be easily absorbed into the intestinal mucosal lining. As soon as this hydrolyzed form gets through the intestinal wall, it recombines with the fatty acids to form esters once again. The portal vein then conveys these esters to the liver where they are stored until the body requires the vitamin for specific maintenance. When it comes time for A to be transported, the blood stream makes available to the liver a particular protein in its plasma which serves as a carrier for the Vitamin A. This example reinforces the importance of dietary protein, for the presence of these carriers, like other forms of body protein, is contingent on one of the first of Nature's conditions which we discussed early in Chapter One, the intake of the eight essential amino acids. [10]

There is another way to get Vitamin A to the epithelium. We speak of A in certain vegetables such as carrots and sweet potatoes, but these foods do not contain retinol. They contain *carotene.* This reddish, crystalline pigment is a provitamin, i.e., a vitamin precursor; and — note this carefully, for it is often overlooked — it cannot be absorbed through the intestinal wall and converted into retinol *unless there are fats and bile salts in the system.*[11] Though the amount of retinol produced by carotene is uneven, a really potent carotene molecule may produce as much as two molecules of retinol.[12]

One last note: current popular literature on the subject isolates the eyes as an object of retinol's nourishment. The eyes are hollow organs, and therefore contain a lining of epithelium susceptable to retinol's action. There is a special enzymatic conversion which is unique there. The seven thousand rods of the eye contain rhodopsin, a protein which can only be stabilized by retinol; the one hundred thirty thousand cones in the eye also contain a pigment which likewise requires retinol, though the vitamin's precise purpose here remains obscure.[13]

Since retinol is an organic alcohol it has all the characteristics of a fatty acid including the tendency to become rancid. It is wise, therefore, whenever taking vitamin A to take Vitamin E at the same time. The alpha tocopherol (Vitamin E) has a sparing effect both on retinol and carotene and are more effective in the system when Vitamin E is ingested at the same time. As we have already observed, E also preserves the oils which all the fat soluble vitamins need to work in the body.

The foods rich in Vitamin A are listed in Section A in the appendix. These may be included in the menus given in Chapters One through Three.

Currently there is probably too much concern in certain quarters about the toxic effects of too much Vitamin A. Over the years, our experience has turned up barely a handful of people suffering from such toxic effects, e.g. nausea, dizziness, and falling hair. In each case, these people had been taking between 50,000 to 100,000 Units daily for a period of three to six months, even a year's time. When they stopped taking such massive doses on a regular basis, the toxic effects disappeared and normal functions resumed.

Increased bodily stress caused by toxicity in our air, food, and water requires us to protect and reinforce our bodily functions with well balanced co-enzymatic support. Through a steady consumption of co-enzymes based on sound scientific principles, we can take a major step toward defeating toxicity and renewing our body ecology.

THE FIBRIN PROJECT

You'll recall we spoke of the organs lined with epithelium and mucosal cells. It is in the mucosal cells of the small intestines that the body begins another project, manufacturing millions of essential friendly bacteria, micro-organisms commonly called flora. From these micro-organisms emerges Vitamin K.[15] K is the only vitamin which we know the body itself can manufacture. For the purpose of entering into an important, extremely complex enzyme system,[16] four steps occur: 1) K passes through the intestinal wall to the liver where it co-synthesizes a protein called *prothrombin.* 2) Prothrombin next unites with calcium salts to synthesize a second protein, *throm-*

bin. 3) Thrombin then unites with still another protein in the blood, *fibrinogen* to produce *fibrin.* 4) Whenever bleeding occurs in the body, fibrin links with the blood cells to form clots.[17] This cycle producing thrombin is one of the most critical protein syntheses in the body, for its aim is to protect the life of the blood. If Vitamin K is not present in the initial stages of this process, clotting time can either decline or fail altogether,[18] causing increased bleeding and multiple hemorrhages throughout all the tissues.

Though the work of K is easily and briefly stated, this in no way minimizes its importance, and liberal food amounts should be taken daily. The most common form is K1 (phylloquinone) found in the vegetables listed in Section A of the Appendix. Another form, K2 (farnoquinone), somewhat less common, is found in putrefying fish meal. Both of these natural sources of Vitamin K are biologically active,[19] but even more active is a synthetic form of K, menadione, which may presently be obtained in liquid or tablet form by prescription only.

THE CALCIFICATION PROJECT

The vitamins discussed up to now have all contributed to processes which either synthesize protein or sustain proteinous substances. But there is a vitamin which uses protein to service another biological function, *calcification.* Calcification is the process of getting calcium to the parts of the body which need it. In Chapter One we spoke about the importance of eating protein and minerals together, offering the reason that it is protein that moves the minerals through the body. The enzyme system that does this requires a special co-enzyme, Vitamin D. Vitamin D originates from a group of substances in the body called sterols. Sterols, by definition, are a group of alcohols which help synthesize various body compounds: hormones, bile acids, and, of course, the D Vitamins. There are anywhere from ten to sixteen sterol derivatives given the collective name of D.[20] And here is something few people realize: These derivatives are all interchangeable and chemically related to cholesterol. A Vitamin D provitamin, for example, 7-dehydrocholesterol, is only four hydrogen atoms away from cholesterol:

$$C_{27}H_{41}OH = 7 \text{ dehydrocholesterol}$$
$$C_{27}H_{45}OH = \text{Cholesterol}$$

When the provitamin is treated (irradiated) with ultra-violet light, it becomes Vitamin D3, cholecalciferol. In nature this happens when our bodies are exposed to sunlight. The ultra-violet rays convert dehydrocholesterol to the biologically active form, cholecalciferol, that is, a sterol (-erol) related to cholesterol (chole-) that can act as a calcifying agent (calcif-) by transporting calcium and phosphorus to the bones.

Let's look at the action of Vitamin D in the intestine. Here its presence increases calcium's rate of diffusion through the mucosal lining of the intestinal wall by triggering the synthesis of a protein which carries the calcium straight through the wall into the blood stream. This, of course, raises the level of the calcium in the blood, making it more available for deposit in the bones. Without the critical triggering action of Vitamin D on the carrier protein, however, there would be no active transport of calcium to its destination. [23]

We'll discuss the bones further in the next chapter, but for the present suffice it here to underscore the importance of Vitamin D's critical function in the adult body by stating that the composition of bone — calcium phosphate, calcium carbonate, magnesium phosphate, and calcium fluoride [24] — must be maintained through the intake of dietary calcium, supplemented with adequate amounts of protein and Vitamin D. In several recorded cases of low dietary calcium, Vitamin D has been able with the help of adequate protein to distribute calcium economically throughout the body. This kind of biochemical environment is not ideal, and, of course, in cases of inadequate dietary calcium, sufficient amounts of the mineral should be restored as soon as possible.

This concludes the vitamins connected primarily with the metabolism of protein. We will consider the B complex activity specifically with protein at the close of the chapter. We do not deny that other vitamins also have related metabolic functions, some of which we know about already, and some of which we are still discovering, nor do we deny that the vitamins we have just considered are themselves involved in other biological activities. Rather we have attempted to bring a certain group of vitamins into focus by stressing their associations with the first of the macronutrients. We will consider a few of these same vitamins and some additional ones in the next group of co-enzymes under discussion. These include Vitamins A, K, D, E, and B, instrumental in the metabolism of oils.

Up to this point we have emphasized the vitamins as agents serving the nutrients, but we must point out that in at least three cases, the nutrients serve the vitamins to enable them to perform separate functions in the body. In the cases of the fat soluble vitamins A, D, and K, for example, essential fats and bile acids enable A to maintain the health of epithelial tissue, enable D to transport calcium through the intestinal wall, and enable K to initiate the body's blood clotting mechanism. Yet there is scattered evidence that the vitamins may return the services rendered to them by the fats and oils by preventing or neutralizing some of the poisonous by-products of fat metabolism.

One probable method Vitamin A uses to protect the rhodopsin in the eye is to neutralize acetone. In the oxidation of acetylaldehyde, Vitamin D might be partially responsible for neutralizing acetic acid's pickling effect on the tissues. Vitamin K may work with two water soluble B vitamins, folic acid and biotin, to prevent the building up of alcohol in the body during fat metabolism. Since there is little research material on this aspect of vitamin activity, the probabilities still remain just that. However, Vitamin E's incontestable anti-oxidant qualities are especially valuable in the final stages of fatty acid oxidation. The peroxides which form must be reduced to water. This is accomplished, as we have seen previously, by the removal of oxygen by Vitamin E. Though this may seem insignificant, it is crucial to any reduction process. This most controversial anti-oxidant prevents the accumulation of peroxides in the cells. Research has shown that much of the aging process is due to premature cell breakdown from peroxide rancidity. In addition, if rancid fat collects in the blood stream, clots may occur causing thrombosis. The oxygen which E preserves is carried to the cells that most require it. There is still much to be learned about Vitamin E, for its action is not well understood. We can make a few additional generalized statements about its anti-oxidant nature, however, which extends to all tissues. First, it appears to work specifically with those enzyme systems transporting oxygen to muscles and active metabolizing tissue such as the endocrines.[30] Secondly, it seems to require the oxidative co-enzymes from active muscle meats. Thus, the areas of the body which are associated with E include the active muscle and endocrine systems. Any activity requiring the conservation and efficient transport of oxygen (in these days of pollution, what activity does not?) certainly requires the support of Vitamin E, which is why athletes as well as smokers are advised to take large amounts of Vitamin E. Especially dramatic are the photographic records of Vitamin E applied to first and second degree burns, i.e., severe epithelial oxidations. Within a few months, the tissue was fully repaired and functioned as normally as before the burns occurred.[31]

Regardless of all speculations, some of which may conflict with others, one fact must be remembered:

for any function they perform in the body, A, D, E, and K need the bile salts and the fats of the body in order to work successfully. *Insufficient fatty acids in the body impair the proper care and maintenance of body protein, especially the epithelium and the mucosal lining through which amino acids are absorbed, as well as the manufacture of prothrombin and globulin protein carriers.*

Once again we see a demonstration that nothing works alone in the body. Each of the active co-enzymes depend on each other and on the enzymes activating them to accomplish specific bodily functions.

— WHERE THE FATS AND CARBOHYDRATES MEET —

Accumulated body fat, commonly known as adipose tissue, is in triglyceride form, i.e., each molecule consists of three parts stearic acid and one part glycerine.[26] Overweight is due to an excess of triglyceride molecules circulating in the cells— specifically in the subcutaneous and mesentery— and when the cells are unable to burn up the triglycerides as fast as they accumulate, the body becomes overweight. This places serious stress on many of its critical organs, most notably the heart and the liver. Remember: *After the fatty acids pass through the intestinal wall they are reunited with glycerine in the lymph stream. From there the new body fat enters directly into the heart through the thoracic duct and the neck veins.*[27] An excessive or sudden influx of fat, therefore, can overtax the heart. The liver must

feverishly continue to convert glucose into triglycerides so fat may be stored in the proper depots and
not congest the lymphatics or the blood stream.[28] It
does so by first combining three molecules of glucose
and removing sixteen parts of oxygen to make stearic
acid:

$$C_6H_{12}O_6$$
$$C_6H_{12}O_6 \quad \ldots \text{(Three molecules of glucose)}$$
$$C_6H_{12}O_6$$
$$\overline{\phantom{C_6H_{12}O_6}}$$

$$C_{18}H_{36}O_{18}$$
$$- O_{16} \ldots \text{(minus sixteen parts oxygen)}$$
$$\overline{\phantom{C_{18}H_{36}O_{18}}}$$

$$C_{18}H_{36}O_2 \quad \ldots \text{(Stearic Acid)}$$

To three of these stearic acid molecules the liver will
add one molecule of glycerine to form a triglyceride.
This occurs after the oxygenases, hydrogenases, and
carboxylases with the help of B1, B2, and B3 split
glucose into lactic acid (cf p. 63). When the liver
replaces two of the hydrogen atoms in the molecular
structure of the lactic acid, the result is glycerine.

$$C_6H_{12}O_6 \quad \ldots \ldots \text{Glucose split into}$$
$$C_3H_6O_3 \quad \ldots \ldots \text{Lactic Acid}$$
$$+H_2 \quad \ldots \ldots \text{plus two hydrogen atoms}$$
$$\overline{}$$

$$C_3H_8O_3 \quad \ldots \ldots \text{Glycerine}$$

This combination of glycerine and stearic acid moves
constantly around the body from the fat depots to
the liver to the cells and so forth.[29] If the liver is
unable to convert the circulating triglycerides into

glucose, the triglycerides will return to the fat depots, thus snowballing the amount of fat which accumulates.

It is thought that the B Complex factor which the cell needs to initiate the burning action of stearic acid is inositol. If this is true, an increased intake of saturated fats therefore would indicate the necessity for additional dietary inositol, either in foods, tablet, or powder form. On the other hand, an increased intake of unsaturated fatty acids— linoleic, linolenic, arachadonic— indicates the necessity for additional dietary choline and B6, since choline is the B vitamin which the cells need to initiate the oxidation of linoleic acid, and B6 is a co-enzyme in transforming linoleic into arachadonic acid, the biologically active form.

The co-enzymeatic activity involved in the metabolism of carbohydrates belongs, as we have seen, almost exclusively to members of the B Complex family. (Review the carbohydrate reduction chart, pp. 63, 96). Our intention here is to indicate the manner in which the Vitamin B complex, serving as a system of co-enzymes, aids and abets the production of energy.

— SWINGING FULL CIRCLE —

We began with the co-enzymes which figured in the metabolism of protein. We are going to swing back now into a similar consideration by describing how several of the B Complex vitamins also serve in the formation of certain body proteins. The B complex is an extraordinary family of co-enzymes, extending its influence along the metabolic pathways of all three basic nutrients.

THE DNA PROJECT

The B Complex is the only group of co-enzymes whose family contributes to the life-giving secret of cell rebirth. A description of this consists of the other half of the protein story related in Chapter One. The Nucleic acids have their own metabolic pathways, and the result is the perpetuation of the very secret of life.

Recall the food protein molecule, the largest food molecule that can be consumed. The nitrogen in that molecule will react with the enzymes in our digestive and metabolic systems to break apart into its basic components, the amino and nucleic acids. In Chapter One we told the first half of the story, tracing the breakdown of protein into amino acids. We followed their path through the intestinal wall to the liver which distributes them throughout the body. Now we'll trace the nucleic acids released from the protein.

In the small intestine, nucleic acids break up into 1) ribose, a sugar with five carbon atoms; 2) phosphoric acid; and 3) four other important elements called *the nitrogen bases*. Herein lies the secret of life, its very source. According to nature's first law, these nitrogen bases are separated so they can be reassembled in the cells as *new* body molecules. The four nitrogen bases are *adenine*, *quanine*, *cytosine*, and *thymine* (or sometimes *urasil*).

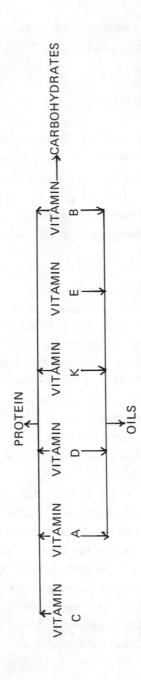

FIG. 21: Classification of Vitamins According to their Co-Enzymatic Function with the Three Basic Nutrients: Protein, Oils and Carbohydrates.

Once again, the liver is the distributing agent, sifting and parcelling out all the elements. Once they arrive in the cells, the sugars, the phosphoric acid, and the four nitrogen bases all arrange themselves in a most fascinating way. We can trace their amazing step by step formation into what will become the chief executive force of life in the cell's nucleus. First, the ribose sugars and the phosphoric acid line up in an alternating fashion, like so:

P S P S P S P S P S P S P S
P S P S P S P S P S P S P S

These two parallel lines of sugars and phosphoric acid serve as the sides of a ladder. The rungs of this ladder are formed by the nitrogen bases, adenine, guanine, cytosine, and thymine. Once they are all assembled and in place, these rungs become what are commonly known as *genes:*

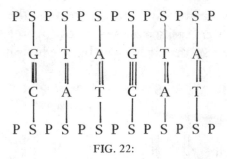

FIG. 22:

Nature then twists the ladder into a helix— a spiral —with the genes containing all the information about the cells coded and stored in astronomical series of combinations.

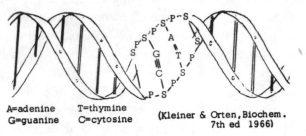

A=adenine   T=thymine
G=guanine   C=cytosine   (Kleiner & Orten, Biochem.
7th ed 1966)

FIG. 23:

This helix exercises executive power over the entire body. In an astounding feat, it *bisects* itself:

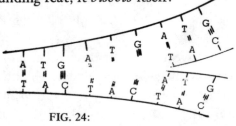

FIG. 24:

The bottom half of this bisection will serve as a messenger for the top half, carrying the genetic code from cell to cell. And so it detaches itself completely and moves on its way. Soon thereafter, the top half of the ladder easily restores itself by reproducing another side so that it is right back where it started:

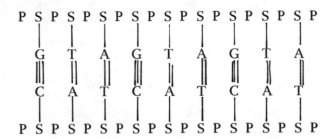

The little messenger, meanwhile, will remain as he is,

one side with rungs. His name is RNA, that is, RiboseNucleic Acid— or, if you'd rather not get tongue-tied and say it quicker, —*Ribonucleic Acid.* RNA is the telegraphing system relaying the genetic code throughout the body.

The Executive helix from which RNA broke away is called DNA, or Deoxyribonucleic Acid. When we take this word apart, de-oxy-ribo-nucleic-acid, we see that DNA gets its name by way of contrast with its derivative messenger, RNA. Nature takes away (de-) one oxgen atom (-oxy-) from the sugar in the ribo nucleic acid. And so, peculiarly enough, even though the father DNA may come first, he is named after his son. Well, why not, after all, look at all the leg work RNA has to do in the body.

But don't be fooled. It is clearly DNA which bears sole responsibility for the building of new cells. The Amino Acids cannot possibly reassemble themselves until DNA gives the word. Therefore, gravitating around the nucleus of each body cell, waiting for executive orders, is an assembly line of foremen called *ribosomes.* When, and only when, the travelling RNA conveys to the ribosomes the blueprint of the genetic code at the direction of DNA will the ribosomes start construction work by activating the amino acids and stitching them together to make any and all of the body proteins we discussed in Chapter One. [33]

We began this discussion of the DNA and RNA with an eye toward the B Complex. Our intention is to emphasize the importance of the B vitamins by linking them with the metabolism of nucleic and amino acids and the subsequent work of the nitrogen bases in DNA. By using a revised summary diagram to describe the breakdown of *food* nucleoprotein, we can chart the co-enzymatic uses of each of the B Vitamins. The left side of the diagram describes the breakdown of food nucleoprotein into those elements which are reassembled on the right side of the diagram to build body protein. The B Vitamins can be spotted in the general areas where they assist as co-enzymes in the reassembling process. (See p. 158).

The B Complex Vitamins restrict their activity to the right side of the diagram, the building of body protein. They begin at the bottom of the chart with adenine, one of the nitrogen bases. Vitamin B2 is a basic component of the adenine nucleotide.[34] It works with B3 (Niacin) to build active nucleotides and sustain good cell respiration.[35]

Further up, closer to the finished products of Nucleic Acid and body protein, we find B12 and folic acid.[36] Folic Acid's basic action is very simple. It transfers single carbon fragments from one compound to another.[37] But these fragments serve as building units in the body's synthesis of new nucleic acids from the nitrogen bases at the bottom of the chart.[38] Further nucleic action of folic acid, however, has not been clearly established, though it appears to be involved in certain intimate reactions in the cell nucleus.[39] Due to its effect on nucleic acid formation and reaction, however, folic acid has a definite positive effect on the growth and regeneration of cells.[40] B12 continues to work on developed tissue in the body, influencing its growth and repair which started by triggering the synthesis of nucleic acids in the cell. This is especially true in those cells which must constantly reproduce themselves, such as the red blood cells,[41] of which 10,000 die every second.

— HARK YE, ALL VEGETARIANS —

The essential co-operation between B12 and Folic Acid has been noted by several nutritionists who have wisely advised vegetarians who do not eat foods containing thymine, the nitrogen base characteristic of the animal cell, that they will not receive a balance of nucleic acids. B12 is present only in the animal cell because it helps to synthesize its DNA nucleic acids of which thymine is a base. B12 is not present in vegetable nucleic acids, however, which are primarily sources of RNA structures and devoid of the thymine base. Folic acid *is* present in vegetable, however, along with uracil (instead of thymine) which can mask a deficiency of B12 in vegetarians who eat no DNA protein. Since B12 is necessary to build up nucleic acids which form red blood cells in the bone marrow, the vegetarian may have anemia and not know it. Though folic acid can get the red blood cells through their intermediate stages of growth (their adolescence, so to speak), it cannot bring them to maturity as B12 can. The vegetarian can correct his deficiency by adding dairy protein to his diet.

— AND ALSO YE MEAT EATERS —

We know we need the thymine of animal DNA, but we also need an element present in vegetable RNA

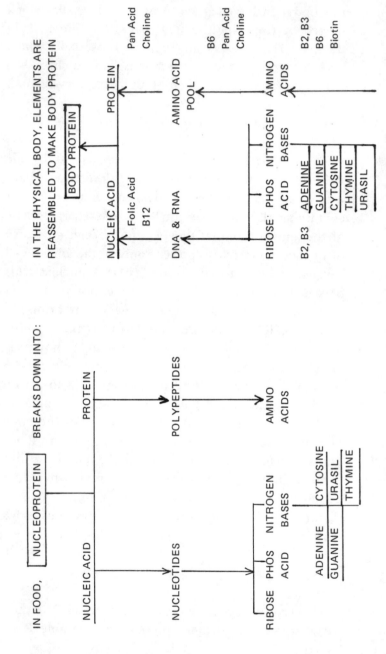

NUCLEOPROTEIN

IN FOOD, NUCLEOPROTEIN BREAKS DOWN INTO:

IN THE PHYSICAL BODY, ELEMENTS ARE REASSEMBLED TO MAKE BODY PROTEIN

FIG. 26: How Food Nucleoprotein is Broken Down into Nucleic and Amino Acids and then Reassembled into Body Protein with co-enzymatic support of the B Complex.

which is *not* present in the animal cell. Nature just insists on balance, and this time it hinges around the ribose sugar. We have said that ribose is a sugar containing five carbon atoms. But the ribose in RNA contains five oxygen atoms as well, whereas the DNA ribose contains only four. Strange as it may seem, we need that extra atom of oxygen in the RNA sugar which is why we must *balance* our meat or fish meals with a sufficient supply of vegetables. Again, it seems, we can't get away from nature's incontrovertible law.

Let's move now to the work of the B Complex vitamins with the amino acids. Biotin, a member of the B Complex family acts as a link between the nucleic and amino acids. It takes a so far unmentioned nucleic acid component, adenylic acid, and uses it to help synthesize certain amino acids with other acids in the body.[42] Biotin works additionally with B2, B3, and B6 to metabolize tryptophane, an amino acid used to detoxify the liver and to maintain and regenerate visual purple. Tryptophane is also a basic component of the red blood cells, the plasma, the brain cells, and at least two digestive enzymes—trypsin and pepsin.

Moving up further in the diagram, we find our old companions choline and pantothenic acid. Choline, we recall, is used in conjunction with the amino acid methionine in the liver's transmethylation process (p. 83). Handling an equally important job, however, choline also passes through the myelin sheaths around the nerves to act as a transmitter of impulses across the nerve synapses and across the closely aligned neuro-muscular junctions.[43] Pantothenic acid, on the other hand, follows glandular directives, and whenever it is required to do so, will remove and help transport hydrogen and oxygen in the same proportion in which they occur in water, The adrenal cortex hormones depend upon this process aided by pantothenic acid.

Perhaps it is difficult to appreciate the importance of the co-enzyme B family when so much must be summed up in such a limited space. Yet the patent versatility of this water soluble complex is ample evidence that without sufficient quantities of it, our carbohydrate and protein metabolism would be severely impaired. Foods containing all of the B vitamins should be plentiful in our diet, especially yeast and liver which contain the complete B complex. (cf Section A in the appendix for more detailed list). There are so many vegetables and fruits to include that you will have little difficulty in selecting B Vitamin foods to serve in the various menus offered in the preceding chapters.

CHAPTER SEVEN:

MINERALS, THE ESSENCE OF THE PLANET WITHIN US

We are about to take a journey through the body. As we observe the harmony of its marvelous organs and structures, let's pay particular attention to the development and function of a group of basic nutrients which extend their life-giving influence into every bone, muscle, nerve, tendon, organ, tissue, and cell in the body. No matter what level we investigate, as atoms become molecules, as molecules become cells, as cells become tissues, as tissues become organs, and as organs become the body, not a single fiber can escape the penetrating mineral essence of our planet. The presence of calcium, phosphorus, magnesium, sodium, potassium, and iron are all major conditions of our interior environment. Let's begin our journey where life itself begins— in the bones.

— *"THE SOURCE OF THE NILE"* —

We rarely think of the bone as the source of life, yet deep within the marrow of its cavernous layers there is a womb of life. It is protected by the solid mineral accumulations that form the structure of each bone linking with another to become the skeletal framework for the muscles, nerves, and organs, the most elaborate transportation and communication system on the planet.

The composition of the skeletal framework— cranium, spine, scapula, humerus, radius, ulna, metacarpels, clavicle, ribs, pelvis, femur, tibia, and metatarsals— consists of four basic mineral salts: calcium phosphate, calcium carbonate, magnesium phosphate and calcium fluoride.[1] These salts compose about 70% of the bone. Another 18% of the bone consists of our old friend, collagen, while other fractional percentages include mixtures of protein and polysaccharides[2] Here in these bones is ninety percent of all the calcium in the body, and 80% of all the phosphorus. Yet how little of it gets here if we do not fortify the body with adequate amounts of Vitamin D and protein. The body also contributes special enzymes which we've mentioned in earlier chapters— hydrochloric acid to dissolve the calcium, and bile salts to emulsify fats which will eventually form permeable cell walls capable of ushering into the cells calcium and other nutrients. Care must be taken not to interfere with calcium assimilation by consuming an overabundance of phosphorus or magnesium, or by eating too many foods containing oxalic acid (listed in the appendix), and phytate complexes. Deep in the bone marrow where blood is born, the red blood cells— the erythrocytes[3] — are manufactured. Once they mature we can follow them through the medullary canals as they take their place in the crimson stream of life. From this stream, the body's cells, tissues, and organs are fed, built, relieved of wastes, respirated, and repaired, and saved from extinction by the phagocytes who deal death blows to hostile micro-organisms. In fact, if we could be diminished to the size of a micro-organism and could be injected into this *60,000 mile transport system* just as we are, we would be attacked and devoured by an army of phagocytes and antibodies.[4] The body would not recognize us either as a legitimate biological nutrient or a waste product. Thus we must temporarily allow Vitamin D to resynthesize the amino acid composition of one of our own globulins in order to travel undisturbed in the blood stream. In this way we can also render a service to our host, the body, by escorting calcium to certain cells which need it. As we enter the arteries we can catch a last glimpse of our Vitamin D being whisked away by another globulin carrier.

— "MANY TRAVELLERS, MANY VEHICLES" —

We're now moving along with our passenger, calcium, in the midst of thousands of other commuters moving as swiftly and efficiently as we are. The tubes we pass through are generally smooth, but occasionally we run into a congested area. Our passage is narrowed because the walls are thickened

inside with mineral salts and cholesterol accumulations. Some of them are so thick that our passenger
may get caught on these fatty protrusions. We make
it through fairly well, but it is somewhat alarming
when we consider that if peroxides get into those
fatty accumulations there could be serious trouble.

Gradually though we get through to a cleaner area,
and as we do, we can get a better look at some of our
fellow travellers: glucose, ketone bodies, uric acid,
cholesterol, iron, amino acids in various stages of
living and dying, lecithin, lactic acid, sodium chloride,
other globulins like ourselves carrying calcium, hormones, vitamins, and lots of minerals, some of which
are already going to work here in the blood. Others,
just getting a free ride, are on their way to the cells.
There is an enormous amount of solids moving along,
and we can see that right next to us, one of the
minerals we are especially interested in, phosphorus,
is busy regulating the hydrostatic pressure so that our
mode of transportation does not become too
gummy.[5]

Another mineral, sodium, is maintaining osmotic
pressure in the plasma,[6] while potassium, the other
half of the balancing team maintains the plasma's
acid-alkali balance.[7]

Suddenly an emergency occurs. Further up, the
body has suffered a laceration in the epidermis.
Though our calcium passenger remains, other calcium
particles rush to the surface along with Vitamin K
particles to join the thrombin proteins. They begin
the coagulation process. Within two minutes enough

fibrin is produced to start sealing the wound so that the healing process may build new epidermal cells.[8]

The tube we are traveling in at this time is the pulmonary artery. We are part of the blood stream which some time ago left the right side of the heart for the lungs to absorb oxygen.[9, 10]

Beneath us we can feel, stretched out, the winding bronchial tubes gradually narrowing into their smaller branches, the bronchi. Eventually all the red blood cells dwindle into a single file procession as we pass cell by cell into a microscopic net of capillaries covering the tiny air sacks — *250,000,000 of them altogether* — at the ends of the bronchioli. How immeasurably enriched we become as through the most gossamer of membranes each red blood cell exchanges its carbon dioxide for fresh oxygen. A few problems can arise here as we get older. Some of the blood cells begin to lose their electrical polarity and become electrically neutral. As a result, they no longer repel each other as they should, and instead they begin to cluster together in a manner that resembles a cluster of grapes. As these unseparated cells pass through the lungs for aeration, only the cells on the outside of the bunch get oxygen. The cells inside remain unaerated. A little niacin, however, will restore the electrical polarity to the blood cells and invest the life stream with new vigor.[11] Our newly aerated stream turns a rich red as we reconvene in the pulmonary vein and sweep speedily along to the heart. [12, 13]

– "IN THE HALL OF THE MOUNTAIN KING" –

We enter this extraordinary and strongest muscle of the body on the left side and pass from the atrium chamber to the ventricle chamber. The decisive thrusts which move us along come from the self-generated energy of this muscle.[14] Its astonishing strength depends largely on two minerals, magnesium and potassium. While magnesium conditions the normal activity of this muscle which works harder than any other in the body, potassium is responsible for transmitting electrical impulses.[15] Without these two indispensable minerals the heart would be stilled and our life-giving stream would cease to flow. Those electrical impulses push us up through the aortic valve[16] and pump us rapidly to the organs of the body awaiting our nutrition.

The rate of our flow through the arteries, the narrower arterioles, and the hairlike capillaries is just enough to supply the exact amount of nutrition required by the organs of the body. As we flow along the neuromuscular sheaths, it so happens we lose our calcium passenger. He slips suddenly, quietly away through the protective myelin sheath around the nerve cells, joining the other nutrients— lecithin and the B complex vitamins— which feed and tone the nerves.

All of the minerals working along this fascinating, intertwining neuromuscular terrain must do double duty. Calcium, for example, must not only feed the nerves to protect them against hyperirritability,[17] but it must also make its way to the muscles to promote contraction and relaxation. Phosphorus, already promoting muscular tone and structure, must also serve as a type of accelerator control of the entire autonomic nervous system. This includes reactions in the glands, the smooth muscles, the heart, and all of the body's reflex controls. Still another important worker, magnesium, not only conditions the normal activity of the nerves, but also stores itself deep in the skeletal muscles to promote the necessary stimuli for muscular control and to protect these muscles against spasms.

We can see sodium and potassium at work as well. Dynamically involved on the level of electrical impulses in steady, preconscious designs still unplotted by scientific studies, sodium stimulates muscles and nerves so they can react according to normal patterns. Potassium, meanwhile, continues to transmit electrical impulses and serves as a transfer agent for enzymes in the neuromuscular system.

The complex activity and cooperation among these elemental mineral workers is astonishing. The laws they obey make it possible for us to build and sustain our lives with newer and more sophisticated forms of energy. And yes, these new forms then become dependent on the service of the minerals.

As we continue our journey, we not only distribute nutrition throughout the body, but we continually pick up enormous amounts of waste material. This waste must be filtered out to purify the blood for its continued use as a transport system. The time for unloading must be near, for we are heading for the master chemist of the body, the kidneys.

Preparing us for the experience, some of our fellow proteins, the albumins, have been gathering all sorts of materials around them. The albumen family is so concentrated in the blood that they attract fluid from the body's cells into the blood stream. This fluid contains dissolved waste such as urea, uric acid, creatinine, and carbon dioxide, resulting from cellular breakdown. Thanks to albumen's magnetic power, the blood can help clean up the cells by collecting the waste products for excretion, an operation reserved for the filtering action of two bean shaped organs, each about the size of a fist, located on either side of the lower spine.

As we enter the kidneys, we are overwhelmed by the number of filtering depots, inside — well over a million! But there's not much time to count, for we are immediately ushered into one of these *nephrons*. The first compartment we find ourselves in is a bulb-like capsule [18] where the filtering process begins. Almost all of us travelling in the crimson stream are absorbed from the capsule into a long, rodlike membrane called a *tubule*. Here we are suspended in a semi-clear liquid called the filtrate, much like plasma, except, since we see fewer of our nitrogenous companions, it is lower in protein. There are actually seventy miles of tubules in the kidneys, but thankfully, we'll only have to travel a fraction of that distance.

About all that is left in the blood moving through

the vessels twisted and curled around the *outside* of our tubule is a heavy concentration of red blood cells. To lessen their concentration according to the law of mass action, these red blood cells will soon begin to reabsorb many of us back into their stream.[19] Already through the membrane walls we witness the first departures. Glucose and water are among the first to return to the blood stream.[20] Now the amino acids begin to pass through, and we see we are going to be among them. As we pass through the membrane walls, we notice a good deal of jostling between the sodium and potassium left behind in the filtrate. The kidneys in cooperation with the pituitary gland carefully regulate the balance of these two minerals through a specific and very rigid transport mechanism, which is as carefully controlled as our own transport mechanism,[21] one which is carried out in conjunction with the filtering process *twice every hour of our lives.*

We have returned to the blood stream now, passing into one of the veins for transport to the heart, where a little short of oxygen, we'll be pumped out to the lungs to be aerated again to renew our cycle.

During our journey, we have seen how extremely important the minerals are, yet frequently we have seen mineral deposits collected in the arteries and in the joints. We have observed that enough free amino acids passing through the blood stream will pick up some of the calcium deposits and get them to the cells where they belong. Yet there is still abundant collections of inorganic calcium in areas where calcification performs no metabolic purpose. These deposits result from poor chelation processes.

To understand the chelation process we must first be acquainted with the problem of mineral absorption. Mineral salts, as we take them, are inorganic substances possessing *positive and negative electrical charges.* When the mineral salts reach the intestine, the positive charges or *cations* dissociate from the negative charges or *anions.* According to the chemical law of polarity, opposite charges attract and similar charges repel, with the result that the mineral anions pass through the intestinal wall quite easily since the intestinal wall is negatively charged and there is nothing to attract or hold the mineral from passing through the pores of the wall. The mineral cation, on the other hand, has a more difficult time. Much of it inclines to stick to the intestinal wall because it is held by the attraction of the wall's negative charge. Whatever part of the mineral remains behind will never reach the bloodstream. It will eventually be excreted with the waste products in the feces.[22] *As much as four-fifths of the cations taken as inorganic salts are lost, with less than one-fifth ever absorbed into the blood stream.*[23] Is it any wonder, then, that we see fewer minerals than we expect accompanying us on our journey? If the inorganic minerals taken into our bodies were organically complexed or chelated, the absorption, research proves, would be vastly improved. To make new red blood cells, bones must be supplied with calcium, magnesium, manganese, zinc, copper, and sulfur by way of *amino acid carriers which, according to the most recent discoveries, constitute the most efficient chelates.*[24] Think of the increased efficiency of a mineral, for example, when it is chelated with lysine to serve as a building block of a new matrix structure, or with methionine which is instrumental in furnishing sulfur as a precursor of collagen formation. [25]

The very medium we are travelling in, the blood, has a history of chelation. Various minerals have acted as catalyzers and exchanged places with one another in a continuing chain of intercellular re-actions to aid in the birth of new blood cells in the bone marrow — where we began this journey. Calcium and magnesium, for example, increase in proportion to the ribonucleic acid as it develops the new cells. These two minerals link phosphates with the ribonuclecic acid. Then, as the immature red cells lose their nuclei, the hemoglobin develops rapidly into polypeptide chains. [26] Next, iron becomes at-tached to the combination of nitrogen and organic acid present in the chain, and finally, another mineral, cobalt, increases the utilization of the iron, but unlike the calcium which always remains a constituent of the red cells (it was not always thought so), cobalt retires from the hemoglobin molecule after stimulating its synthesis. [27] And all of this is what must ensue if the lifestream is to spring forth from the heart of our bones.

— SHOOTING TO THE TOP
FOR THE BEST VIEW —

The very formation of the life-carrying blood cell itself is dependent on the enzymatic, catalyzing functions of the minerals. And yet, a final vision of the minerals, and perhaps the source of their most amazing work remains to be seen. To get the best perspective, let's continue our journey by leaving the bloodstream and latching onto one of those millions of electrical impulses shooting along the spinal nerve "wires" up to the brain. The outer surface of the brain, a yard long and two feet wide in size, is a sheet of gray colored cells crumpled up into a densely packed hilly terrain, each hill separated by deep, narrow gullies. This organ, a little larger than two fists placed together, besides turning light and sound impulses into useful electrochemical patterns, monitors and controls the actions of the entire body. Encased in the skull, the brain floats in a protective pool of clear fluid which cushions it against shock. [28] *This fluid is part of a marvelous tide that bathes, inside and out, all the cells of the body.* Outside the cells, there are two kinds of fluid: *interstitial fluid and plasma.* Interstitial fluid bathes the cells outside the blood vessels, while plasma bathes the cells inside the blood vessels. [29] The plasma is part of the transport system that carries red blood cells through the body and speeds the white cells to attack bacteria. As we have seen, the plasma's pick-up and delivery system includes such items as food, fuel, gases, vitamins, minerals, enzymes, and hormones. The plasma also sorts out numerous body nutrients for storage and carries off the wastes for disposal. The interstitial fluid likewise transports enzymes and hormones and replenishes those cells that secrete saliva, mucous, tears, bile, and digestive juices. But most important, these bodily fluids consist of a solution of water and dissolved minerals or *salts.* In water, salts or *electrolytes*, generate tiny electrical charges called ions. These ions, as we explained in the section on chelation are either positively or negatively charged. The positive electrolytes, or cations, include sodium, potassium, calcium, and magnesium. The negative electrolytes, or anions, include chloride, bicarbonate, sulfate, phosphate, proteinate, and carbonic acid. [30] As the mineral charged waters move in and out of the cells they create a vital climate for their sustained life. This osmosis or transport of ions moving through cell membranes from areas of lesser ionic concentration to areas of greater ionic concentration requires energy from a source *yet unknown*. But again, following the law of mass action, the areas with a heavier concentration of minerals will always draw water from the areas with a lighter concentration of minerals. And so, in and out, permeating the cells, tissues and organs, flows the tide of life-supporting ions. As we shoot along the nerve impulses from synapse to synapse along the spinal cord, we can feel the support of that interstitial ocean beneath us, and we can see its tributaries moving ever so slowly through the body's membraneous geography, exchanging ions for ions, life for life.

And thus it goes. Throughout our explorations of the physiology and biochemistry of the body, the single principal of balance and exchange persists. The intricate and astonishing ways by which it sustains life are often microscopically elusive, yet at other times, they are so organically extensive that the effect is overwhelming. To retain the completeness of the body, and to sustain its health and longevity is fundamentally to serve its principle of balance and exchange. Even though digestion and metabolism are complicated and at times even impossible to unravel,

an understanding of their activity elicits a responsibility from us to employ practical means to respect and
preserve their secrets. If we abuse nature with
stressful conditions, starve her with inadequate fuel
sources, irritate and poison her with chemical and
toxic substances, we will reap the sad harvest. So
many of us, regretfully, instead of engaging nature in
an exchange of life-giving energy, end up involving
her in an enigmatic conflict which destroys the
harmonious life of service which man and nature
render to each other. With proper nutrition we can
nurture and sustain growth and evolution. The
acknowledgment and understanding of nature's law
of balance and exchange within us will prepare us for

FINALE:

ALL TOGETHER, NOW

In the preceding chapters we have analysed the
basic nutrients and their important co-workers in
digestion and metabolism. Along the way there have
also been some lessons in anatomy and physiology.
Any thorough analysis, however, leaves the subject
analysed in chunks that should be reassembled in
order to see the complete picture. What we will do
here, then, is capsulize the nature of balanced
nutrition by combining the scientific facts of digestion and metabolism with the practical application
of the menus.

The purpose of balanced nutrition is the production of healthy cells. We eat, after all, to feed our cells and give forth energy. In the body, Nature, who must break apart the component parts of one form in order to build another, breaks down food cells in digestion and builds new body cells through the complicated pathways of metabolism. Thus food protein becomes body protein; food fat becomes body fat; and carbohydrate or food sugar becomes glucose or blood sugar.

The body breaks the food protein down into amino and nucleic acids which make up both the cell's protoplasm and its nucleus where the reproductive blueprint for all the cells of the body is stored. For this absorption to take place, we must eat complete protein foods which contain the eight essential amino acids so that our bodies can manufacture from them the other sixteen. These essential amino acids must be taken together at the same meal in foods which supply them in a ratio suitable for complete assimilation. They are found in eggs, milk, fish, poultry, cheese, and meat. Each menu in the preceding chapters is centered around a complete protein food, unless otherwise stated. Some of the amino acids derived from these complete protein foods will link with body fat to form a substance called lipoprotein which constitutes the porous cell wall. Through this cell wall pass the nutrients which build, maintain, and repair the cell. For example, only a small percentage of body fat combines with amino acids to form cell walls. Most body fat, a combination of fatty acid and glycerine, passes through the cell wall into the protoplasm where it combines with oxygen and burns to create energy. Glucose follows the same pathway, likewise passing through the cell wall into the protoplasm for oxidation.

It is up to us to maintain a balanced intake of protein, fats and carbohydrates at each meal so that all of these complementary metabolic actions can occur. Our cells depend for their very life on a balanced supply of the amino and nucleic acids, fatty acids, and glucose derived from the protein, fats, and carbohydrates in our food. A balanced program provides normalized weight and maximum heat and energy. A "recommended daily allowance" for each of the basic food nutrients includes:

PROTEIN: 60-75 grams, approx.
FATS IN THE FORM OF POLYUNSATURATED OILS: 2-3 Tbsp. approx.
CARBOHYDRATES: (3-4 oz. approx. serving per meal)

Important for digesting protein such as eggs, milk, fish, meat, grains, nuts and seeds, are the stomach enzymes hydrochloric acid and pepsin. These extremely important enzymes initiate the digestion of protein in the stomach, and if they become scarce they must be replenished as quickly as possible. Pancreatic enzymes and the intestinal enzymatic juices then complete the release of free amino acids and nitrogen bases.

The most scientific way to balance fats so they do not put extra pounds on us is to combine the saturated fats with polyunsaturated oils, especially safflower oil which contains the essential linoleic acid. This provides for maximum assimilation, transmethylation, and oxidation. Fats so balanced should be eaten along with protein so that some of the amino and fatty acids can combine in the body to form the porous lipoprotein membranes of the cell walls. The nuts and seeds discussed in the preceding chapters are not only eminently nutritious since they contain both the polyunsaturated oils and the high quality protein, but they are more efficiently assimilated when they are prepared by the methods we have suggested. (Cf. Breakfast Menu, #3)

Moderation in eating fats is extremely important. The liver already has enough work to do (400 daily activities that we know of) without making the job tougher by congesting it with an oversupply of saturated fatty acids so tough to transmethylate that the liver must either allow some to accumulate to form fatty tissue around its lobes or let some spill into the blood stream where the fatty particles are apt to harden along the inside of the arteries. If we are to remain in good health and maintain our normal weight, we will sensibly balance our fats and oils first with each other, and secondly with the other nutrients — proteins and carbohydrates — so that they can be used efficiently as metabolites.

As long as the individual's requirements for protein and polyunsaturated oil are fulfilled at each meal, a sufficient amount of carbohydrates in the form of fruits and vegetables may be taken *to satisfy hunger and complete the meal.* This may be done, as we have

specified in the menus, with fruits and vegetables —
and we repeat, without the danger of putting on extra
pounds. This should *not* be done with bread and
cereal and the heavily saturated nuts (pecans,
cashews, brazils, etc.). These carbohydrates *will* put
on extra pounds if their amounts are not rigidly
controlled. No matter when bread and cereals are
eaten they should always be reinforced with protein
and polyunsaturated oil, which is why we insist when
toast is eaten that it be reinforced with the nut-seed
meal; and oatmeal or cream of rye, that it be
reinforced with safflower oil, nutseed meal, and
fertile eggs. Again, the balanced reinforcement guards
against metabolic imbalance, and of course, against
overindulgence resulting in overweight. Since the
digestive faculties must reduce all carbohydrates to
the simplest sugar, glucose, we must aid the process
by thoroughly masticating the tough starch forms —
rice, potatoes, bread, corn, bananas — in the mouth,
for here in the saliva ptyalin accomplishes the first
important stages of carbohydrate conversion. If we
remember that two teaspoons of sugar is all the body
can handle at one time, and that a balanced glucose
level in the blood stream is critical to our health, then
we should be more inclined first to reject the highly
concentrated sugars found in processed foods and
second to refrain from long range weight-losing diets
which prohibit the intake of the necessary sugars
from natural fruits and vegetables. Grains in the form
of whole grain breads and cereals are advantageous as
sources of the natural B Vitamins, but if green leafy
vegetables, liver, yeast, or a B supplement are
regularly included in the diet, their presence may be
kept to a minimum and even eliminated without

danger to our health.

The elimination of the solid waste resulting from the digestion of protein, fat, and carbohydrates should be as efficient as the metabolism of these nutrients. For the proper care of the colon, there are basically eight rules to follow:

1) Chew food into a mush before swallowing.
2) Replenish gastric, hepatic, and pancreatic enzymes if enzyme depletion or intestinal congestion occurs.
3) Detoxify the body periodically by setting aside a weekly or monthly day of abstinence in which only juices, beet leaf tea and water are taken.
4) Avoid all foods containing preservatives and any food which irritates the colon, especially regulating the intake of cellulose.
5) Set aside a specific time for elimination and establish a schedule which will support the natural rhythm of the body.
6) Eat foods which facilitate efficient evacuation.
7) Exercise regularly to aerate the blood and move lactic acid out of the muscles.
8) Avoid chemical laxatives and frequent enemas as much as possible, choosing scientific colon therapies wisely and using them only when necessary.

These simple rules will help to adjust minor intestinal irregularities and serve as a general safeguard for colon health.

The balanced intake of protein, oils, and carbohydrates results in the formation of new body tissue

derived from the amino and nucleic acids, and energy
derived from the fatty acids and the glucose. Contributing to body tissue and energy are two groups of
micronutrients: vitamins and minerals. Both of these
micronutrient families should be understood primarily in the light of their metabolic work with
protein, fats, and carbohydrates. All vitamins work
with larger enzyme systems and are therefore called
co-enzymes. Vitamins A, B, C, D, and K, for example,
perform different intermediate functions which require the dietary intake of protein. Transported by
protein carriers to the mucosal layer of the epithelium, Vitamin A is responsible for maintaining the
integrity of the entire epithelial structure by means of
an enzyme process which is still being clinically
explored. The various members of the B Complex aid
in synthesizing first the amino acids which combine
to form body protein and, secondly, the nucleic acids
which combine to form the DNA and the RNA in the
nucleus of each cell. Vitamin C, ascorbic acid, is
extremely versatile: 1) it synthesizes two glandular
secretions, thyroxin and adrenalin; 2) It catalyzes two
amino acids, proline and lysine, to form collagen
which cements all the organs of the body; and 3) It
activates white corpuscles to attack and devour
harmful micro-organisms. Vitamin D triggers the
synthesis of a protein carrier which transports calcium through the intestinal wall into the bloodstream
and then carries it to its destination in the nerves, the
muscles, and the bones. Vitamin K initiates the
synthesis of fibrin, a body protein which supplies the
critical blood clotting factor.

While each of these vitamins performs its co-enzymatic functions with body protein, all but one work additionally with fatty acids in the cell. They depend on the fatty acids chiefly for their individual functions as fat soluble vitamins and as such consequently need Vitamin E, the anti-oxidant co-enzyme, that preserves all fatty acid acitivity in the body.

In the oxidation of fats and carbohydrates, the B Complex truly comes into its own. Its most important components split glucose into lactic acid and form a multimembered enzyme called co-enzyme A which practically bears full responsibility for reducing pyruvic acid to carbon dioxide and water.

The purpose, therefore, of vitamins or co-enzymes, is to increase the efficiency of balanced nutrition. We cannot expect vitamins to perform miracles in our bodies if we think of them as autonomous substances working independently of food. Separated from the macronutrients derived from a balanced intake of eggs, milk, cheese, poultry, meat, fish, polyunsaturated oils, fruits, vegetables, and grains, vitamin activity is wasted.

The sustained life of the cell is the object of all nutrition. This is no less true of the minerals which provide an environment in the cells conducive to the specific metabolic functions we have discussed. The blood, bones, tissues, nerves, muscles, heart, and brain, all need the five major minerals and the trace elements to sustain their metabolism. Calcium, perhaps the most important, has a number of functions: it follows the co-enzymatic activity of Vitamin K by uniting with prothrombin to synthesize thrombin, a protein necessary for blood clotting; it composes a large percentage of the bones; it tones the nerves to prevent them from becoming hyperirritable; it enables the muscles to contract and relax naturally and easily; in fact, all the tissues in the body need calcium to maintain the permeability of all the cellular membranes. Calcium is also the mineral most difficult to assimilate. We need nearly one gram daily, but the presence of the following nutrients must also be present since they function in the absorption of calcium:

1) Hydrochloric acid to dissolve the calcium in the stomach.

2) Polyunsaturated oil to aid the function of Vitamin D.

3) Vitamin D to trigger the protein carriers which transport calcium through the intestinal wall.

4) Ample protein for suitable chelation and to provide protein carriers.

5) Vitamin C, which cannot function in the cell without calcium and which likewise helps to chelate calcium.

7) Magnesium at about one half the amount of dietary calcium for the same reason.

our food. By regulating the hydrostatic pressure in the blood, phosphorus controls the viscosity of the bloodstream. Along with calcium, it forms a large percentage of the bones. Phosphorus serves as an accelerator control for the autonomic nervous system, forms and sustains muscle structure, links with fats and lecithin to form phospholipids necessary for brain cells, and is a critical agent in the production and division of every cell in the body.

Magnesium is everywhere. It forms a small part of the bone structure, and in the muscles it is stored both as an anti-spasmodic and as the source of needed stimuli for muscle control. By means of biochemical processes still not clearly understood, it conditions the normal activity of the brain, the heart, and the nervous system. In all the tissues, magnesium contributes to the cell's production of energy as a co-enzyme activator of B1 in the oxidation of carbohydrates.

Sodium and *potassium,* the brother and sister balancing act usually work together wherever they are found in the body. In the blood plasma, for example, sodium maintains the osmotic pressure, while potassium maintains the alkali balance. In the brain, salts of sodium and potassium are important for the transmission of electrical impulses. Sodium stimulates the neuro-muscular system so it can react to stimuli, while potassium transmits electrical impulses along the neuro-muscular terrain, and one of the most important of these transmissions, of course, takes place in the strongest, most amazing muscle in the body, the heart. In all of the cells of the tissues, sodium is especially responsible for the ionic and water balance of cellular fluids. By means of its drawing power, sodium controls the cell's osmotic pressure; while potassium, remaining one of the chief constituents of intracellular fluids, manages to sustain the water content of the cell due probably to its constant shifting back and forth.

Fruits and vegetables containing vitamins and minerals should be plentifully supplied during the day. The menus recommended specify fruits and vegetables in liberal amounts. A list of these foods enumerating their vitamin and mineral content appears after the weekly menu programs at the close of this chapter, and may be included in the menus wherever fruits and vegetables are specified. A wide variation is recommended, of course, to provide a maximum coverage of vitamins and minerals in the diet. Healthful eating, utilizing the menus already discussed and arranged in weekly programs such as recommended in the pages that follow, or devised by yourself, will probably provide not only more variety than most of us are accustomed to getting in our meals, but will most assuredly provide a balanced supply of protein, fats, and carbohydrates with their co-enzymatic helpers, the vitamins and minerals needed for normal health. With a fundamental knowledge of the science of nutrition and the faithful adherence to sensible, rhythmic eating habits, normal health and weight can be maintained and a majority of malnutritionally-related diseases can be prevented. We may also add that the advisability of including food supplements in tablet or capsule form is a decision which can be made with facility and confidence when such a decision is based on a knowledge of these fundamentals of nutrition. Intelligent, healthful living should be reinforced and complemented by intelligent, healthful eating. The secret is balance, of course, Nature's incontrovertible law.

APPENDIX

SECTION A: FOODS RICH IN THE VITAMINS

VITAMIN C:
Guava
Turnip greens
Broccoli
Kale
Mustard greens
Collards
Brussel Sprouts
Oranges

VITAMIN A:
Liver
Carrots
Turnip greens
Sweet potatoes
Kale
Collards
Mustard greens

VITAMIN A: (cont'd.)
Mangos
Squash
Broccoli
Cantaloupe
Butter
Eggs

VITAMIN K:
Alfalfa
Cauliflower
Spinach
Cabbage
Tomatoes
Kale
Liver

VITAMIN D:
Cod liver oil
Herring
Mackerel
Egg yolk
Raw certified milk

VITAMIN E:
Wheat germ oil
Corn oil
Soy oil
Kale
Meat
Parsley
Eggs
Butter

THE B COMPLEX:

Yeast, liver (entire B Complex)

B1: Soy Beans
Whole Wheat Bread
Oatmeal
Roasted peanuts
Peas
Pecans
Walnuts
Wheat germ
Brown rice
Lima beans

B2: Turnip greens
Mushrooms
Soy beans
Peas
Collards
Kale

NIACIN:

Roasted peanuts
Mushrooms
Brown Rice
Almonds

NIACIN: (cont'd.)

Wheat
Tuna
Turkey
Veal
Chicken
Peas

B6: Whole Wheat
Bananas
Beef liver
Halibut
Molasses
Oranges
Roasted peanuts
Sweet potatoes
Wheat germ

BIOTIN:

Egg
Roasted peanuts
Cauliflower
Mushrooms

CHOLINE:

Egg yolk
Milk
Oats
Green beans
Peanut butter
Peas
Spinach
Wheat germ
Soy beans

INOSITOL:

Cantaloupe
Grapefruit
Oranges
Peas
Raisins
Wheat germ

PANTOTHENIC ACID:

Roasted peanuts
Wheat germ
Soy beans
Mushrooms
Broccoli

PANTOTHENIC ACID: (cont'd.)
Oats
Beef liver
Eggs
Whole wheat
Oranges
Cheese
Chicken
Milk

FOLIC ACID:
Lima beans
Wheat germ
Roasted peanuts
Spinach
Whole wheat
Parsley
Watermelon
Asparagus
Potatoes
Cantaloupe

B12:   Kidney
       Meat

B12: (cont'd.)
Fish
Milk
Cheese
Egg yolk

SECTION B: FOODS RICH IN THE MINERALS

CALCIUM:
Raw certified milk
Cheese
Egg yolk
Molasses
Almonds
Sesame seeds
Brussel sprouts
Collards
Turnip greens

CALCIUM FOODS CONTAINING OXALIC ACID:
Spinach
Rhubarb
Cranberries
Chocolate

MAGNESIUM:
Lima beans
Almonds
Oatmeal
Whole wheat flour
Brown rice
All leafy vegetables
Asparagus

PHOSPHORUS:
Cheese, milk, eggs
All meats, especially beef, turkey
Raisins
Mushrooms
Wheat bread
Oatmeal

PHOSPHORUS: (cont'd.)
Walnuts
Almonds
Rice

SODIUM:
Salted butter
Canned salmon
Cottage cheese
Cheddar cheese
Whole chicken eggs

POTASSIUM:
Molasses
Spinach
Dried fruit, esp. apricots

IRON:
Barley
Liver
Oysters
Bananas
Lima beans
Molasses
Chard

IRON: (cont'd.)
Almonds
Raisins

MANGANESE:
Oatmeal
Whole grain wheat
Whole grain wheat flour
Rye, whole grain
Lettuce
Corn
Bananas
Kale
Beets
Dried prunes
Sweet potatoes
Onions
Liver

COBALT:
Turnip greens
Lettuce
Beet tops
Buckwheat
Cabbage

COBALT: (cont'd.)
Peas
Tomatoes

ZINC:
Bran
Whole wheat
Peas
Rolled oats
Beets
Barley
Carrots
Corn
Peanut butter
Cabbage
Rice
Potatoes
Oranges
Oysters
Liver
Beef
Egg yolk
Clams

CHLORINE:
Olives
Bacon
Oysters
Dates
Kidney
Coconut, dry
Whole wheat flour
Heart
Eggs

CHLORINE: (cont'd.)
Celery
Kale

IODINE:
Iodized salt
Sea vegetation
Fish

The food sources of iodine are so limited, it appears to be the one element which justifies supplementation in microgram quantities.

SULFUR:
Heart
Chicken
Liver
Dried beans
Turkey
Lean beef

SULFUR: (cont'd.)
Salmon
Clams
Lamb
Oatmeal

SECTION C:

Balanced Division of Nutrients by Grams & Calories[1].

Dietary Calories		Carbo- hydrate	Fat	Protein
1000	grams	100	40	60
	calories	400	360	240
1050	grams	105	40	65
	calories	420	360	260
1100	grams	110	45	65
	calories	440	405	260
1150	grams	115	45	70
	calories	460	405	280
1200	grams	125	45	75
	calories	500	405	300
1250	grams	130	50	75
	calories	520	450	300
1300	grams	135	50	75
	calories	540	450	300
1350	grams	145	50	80
	calories	580	450	320
1400	grams	150	50	85
	calories	600	450	340
1450	grams	155	55	85
	calories	620	495	340
1500	grams	165	55	85
	calories	660	495	340
1550	grams	170	55	90
	calories	680	495	360
1600	grams	175	60	90
	calories	680	540	360
1650	grams	180	60	95
	calories	720	540	380
1700	grams	190	60	100
	calories	760	540	400
1750	grams	195	65	100
	calories	780	585	400

Calories		Carbo-hydrate	Fat	Protein
1800	grams	200	65	105
	calories	800	585	420
1850	grams	210	65	105
	calories	840	585	420
1900	grams	215	70	105
	calories	860	630	420
1950	grams	220	70	110
	calories	880	630	440
2000	grams	225	75	110
	calories	900	675	440
2050	grams	230	75	115
	calories	920	675	460
2100	grams	235	75	120
	calories	940	675	480

Analysis of Fatty Acid Composition[2].

	Fatty Acids		
	Total	Unsaturated	
	Sat'd Gms	Oleic Gms	Linol Gms
Almond	4	36	11
Brazilnut	13	32	17
Cashew	8	32	3
Filbert	3	34	10
Pecan	5	45	14
Walnut, black	4	21	28
Walnut, English	4	10	40

1. Courtesy John D. Kirschmann, Nutrition Almanac, Bismarck, N. Dakota, 1972.
2. Courtesy Ford Heritage. Composition and Facts about Food, Health Research, Mokelumne Hill, California, 1968.

SECTION D:

THE SIX MONTH BALANCED MENU SAMPLER.

1ST. MONTH	B'FAST	LUNCH	SUPPER
S	2	2	4A
M	1	1	1A
T	3	20	5
W	7	4	2A
T	9	9	1B
F	2	1	1C
S	8A	3	3A
S	5	8	3
M	2	1	3B
T	1	7	9
W	3	6	2B
T	7	1	1A
F	9	9	4B
S	8B	2	7

2ND. MONTH	B'FAST	LUNCH	SUPPER
S	7	4	1A
M	8B	1	3C
T	3	10	4B
W	9	11	2B
T	2	1	3A
F	1	7	9
S	3	2	1B
S	5	6	2C
M	5	6	2C
T	8A	9	7
W	3	12	1A
T	9	2	4C
F	2	1	1C
S	1	3	8

1ST. MONTH	B'FAST	LUNCH	SUPPER
S	9	5	1A
M	3	3	2C
T	2	1	3C
W	1	11	7
T	3	2	4C
F	8A	9	5
S	7	1	3B
S	6	8	10
M	3	3	8
T	1	1	1B
W	2	2	4A
T	5	12	7
F	3	1	3B
S	9	6	2A

2ND. MONTH	B'FAST	LUNCH	SUPPER
S	3	10	1A
M	4	2	5
T	7	5	3A
W	9	1	7
T	5	3	2A
F	8B	9	4A
S	2	1	1A
S	6	2	3B
M	3	11	2B
T	1	7	10
W	7	1	7
T	9	4	1B
F	2	1	1C
S	3	3	8

3RD. MONTH

Day	B'FAST	LUNCH	SUPPER
S	2	12	1A
M	8A	9	5
T	3	6	7
W	1	1	3C
T	7	5	2A
F	9	2	4B
S	3	1	1B
S	5	10	1A
M	2	11	2B
T	9	4	1C
W	3	12	7
T	1	2	4C
F	7	1	3C
S	9	3	8

Day	B'FAST	LUNCH	SUPPER
S	10	6	1A
M	8B	9	7
T	2	10	8
W	9	5	2A
T	3	1	3A
F	1	7	9
S	7	2	4A
S	6	11	1B
M	8A	4	2B
T	3	9	1C
W	2	2	4B
T	9	3	3B
F	3	1	7
S	1	7	10

4TH. MONTH

Day	B'FAST	LUNCH	SUPPER
S	8B	5	1A
M	3	1	3C
T	4	3	2C
W	9	6	1C
T	2	1	3A
F	5	12	7
S	3	2	4C
S	5	8	1B
M	7	4	2A
T	1	1	3B
W	9	2	7
T	3	10	1A
F	2	1	3C
S	8A	4	4B

Day	B'FAST	LUNCH	SUPPER
S	3	2	3B
M	9	3	8
T	7	5	2B
W	1	1	7
T	3	6	4C
F	9	9	1B
S	2	1	5
S	6	8	3A
M	3	11	2C
T	1	1	1C
W	7	4	4A
T	9	5	1A
F	2	1	3B
S	8B	2	7

5TH. MONTH	B'FAST	LUNCH	SUPPER
S	2	12	5
M	9	9	1B
T	3	6	2A
W	2	10	8
T	7	1	1A
F	1	2	4B
S	9	3	3C
S	5	8	1C
M	2	1	3A
T	9	9	7
W	3	2	4C
T	2	11	2B
F	7	1	1A
S	1	3	8

6TH. MONTH	B'FAST	LUNCH	SUPPER
S	10	10	3B
M	7	2	7
T	1	7	10
W	9	4	4A
T	2	1	1A
F	6	8	2B
S	3	3	3A
S	5	11	2A
M	9	1	1B
T	7	2	4B
W	1	7	9
T	9	3	3B
F	2	1	1C
S	3	12	2C

5TH. MONTH	B'FAST	LUNCH	SUPPER
S	9	4	1C
M	5	2	7
T	2	9	1B
W	4	1	4A
T	3	6	2C
F	8A	3	3B
S	7	1	1A
S	6	8	4B
M	1	7	9
T	9	3	3C
W	2	1	1B
T	5	12	2A
F	3	1	5
S	8B	5	1C

6TH. MONTH	B'FAST	LUNCH	SUPPER
S	3	7	10
M	7	5	1A
T	8B	1	5
W	2	3	2A
T	1	2	4C
F	9	9	1B
S	2	1	3C
S	6	6	7
M	3	1	1A
T	7	4	2B
W	9	9	1B
T	2	2	4A
F	1	10	5
S	5	3	6

SECTION E

PROGRAM FOR REDUCING

The balance of Protein, Oils, and Carbohydrates must be maintained in a reducing regime in order that the body maintain optimum health during the time of weight loss.

The following program is a thousand calorie diet that sustains energy through balanced nutrition:

1,000 CALORIES.

B'FAST:

A) ½ grapefruit
B) 2 soft boiled eggs with
C) 1 tsp. safflower oil (cold pressed)
D) ¼ cup low fat cottage cheese

PROTEIN	23.5 grams
FAT	17.5 grams
CHO	27.5 grams
CALORIES	297

HYDROLYZED AMINO ACID BROTH: (taken with breakfast and as a snack between meals)

2 tsp. amino acid compound in cup of boiling water. (15 gms. protein).
Stir. Drink.
½ tsp. Polyunsaturated oil or its equivalent in one or two essential oil capsules.

LUNCH:

A) 4 oz. of salmon, turkey, chicken, or water packed tuna, mixed with
B) 1 Tbsp. cold processed mayonnaise
C) 1 raw tomato with juice of
D) 1 slice lemon

PROTEIN	34 grams
FAT	21 grams
CHO	6.7 grams
CALORIES	358

HYDROLYZED AMINO ACID BROTH with ½ tsp. Polyunsaturated Oil or its equivalent in one or two essential capsules.

SUPPER:

A) Lean meat (Hamburger, broiled liver, lean round steak, broiled chicken) or fish.
B) Raw vegetable salad
C) 2 tsp. oil with
D) 2 tsp. vinegar

PROTEIN 30.6 grams
FAT 20.3 grams
CHO 4.7 grams
CALORIES 332

SUBSTITUTES:

B'FAST:

A thru D: **THE OATMEAL-RYE RECIPE** (twice weekly)

A: Grapefruit, orange, apple, or tomato juice
B,C,D: Cottage cheese omelet
D: 1 cup plain yogurt

LUNCH:

A & B: ½ cup cottage cheese and two extra essential oil caps with AMINO ACID BROTH.

SUPPER:

B thru D: 2 steamed vegetables, excluding those on the FORBIDDEN LIST (three times weekly if desired) with a raw tomato with oil and vinegar.

FORBIDDEN:

Beans
Peas
Corn
Rice
Potatoes
Whole milk
Cream
Pork,ham
Sausage
Pot roast
Shrimp
Oysters
Cocoa
Candy
Cookies
Cake, pie
Ice cream
Sherbert
Bread

SECTION F

BALANCED VEGETARIAN COOKERY

The foods in all three columns on the following page are deficient in one or more of the essential amino acids, thus each food is an incomplete protein.

The legumes in Column 1 are generally weak in tryptophane and methionine. They are relatively strong, however, in lysine and isoleucine. The grains, nuts, and seeds in column II, however, contain an opposite proportion. They are rich in tryptophane and methionine, but weak in lysine and isoleucine.* Combining foods from Column I with foods from Column II afford a complete amino acid balance. The number following the food represents the number of grams of protein your body can use, not the total number of grams of protein contained in the food.

The vegetables in Column III, on the other hand, are highly variable in their amino acid content. This makes it extremely difficult to depend on any combination of them to gain a balance of the eight essential amino acids.

For additional amino acid analysis, cf. Lappe, Frances Moore, *Diet for a Small Planet,* Tables, pp 78 ff., Ballantine, New York, 1971.

BALANCED VEGETARIAN COOKERY

PROTEIN

I	II	III
LEGUMES	GRAINS, SEEDS, NUTS	VEGETABLES
Soy beans, 11[1]	Whole grain wheat, 5[2]	Green lima beans, 4[3]
Pinto beans, 7	Pumpkin seeds, 5	Green peas
Mung beans, 7	Sunflower seeds, 4	Brussels sprouts, 3
Green peas, 6	Whole grain rye, 4	Corn (1 ear), 3
Black beans, 5	Egg noodles, 4	Broccoli, 2-3
Kidney beans, 5	Barley, 4	Kale, 2
Blackeyed peas, 5	Millet, 3	Collards, 2
Garbanzos, 5	Cashews, 3	Mushrooms, 2
Lima beans, 5	Peanuts, 3	Asparagus, 1.8
Tofu, soybean curd, 5	Sesame seeds, 3	Artichokes, 1.8
Lentils, 4	Black Walnuts, 3	Cauliflower, 1.8
Mung sprouts, 4	Almonds, 3	Turnip greens, 1.4
Navy beans, 4	Oatmeal, 3	Mustard greens, 1.4
White beans, 4	Whole grain rice, 3	Potatoes, 1.4
Wheat germ, 2 weak in tryptophane only	Brazils, 2	
	English Walnuts, 2	
	Pecans, 2	

VEGETARIANS: ALWAYS combine a food from column I with a food from column II to give yourself a complete amino acid balance. This will give you high quality balanced protein, but it may not give you enough quantity. Foods selected from column III may be included in meals which contain combinations from columns I and II thus boosting the protein quantity, but they must NEVER be substituted for foods in either column I or II.

It is even more advisable to add a dairy product at each meal (egg, milk, cottage cheese) to boost the quality and the quantity of protein nutrition, and to improve the balance as well. A complete, well-balanced amino acid broth taken just before the meal is another good way to accomplish the same thing.

The number following a food in Column I represents approximately the number of grams of protein assimilated from that food provided it is combined with a supplementary food in Column II. Likewise, the number following a food in Column II represents approximately the number of grams of protein assimilated from that food, provided it is combined with a supplementary food in Column I.

CARBOHYDRATES: The carbohydrate nutrition in the above foods is sufficient for the meals in which they are included.

OILS: Include at each meal approximately 1 Tbsp. of polyunsaturated oil. Do not neglect this.

(1) Grams of protein per ¼ - 1/3 cup in dry state.
(2) Grains: grams of protein per 3-3½ oz. serving.
Nuts and seeds: grams of protein per oz.
(3) Grams of protein per 3-3½ oz. serving.

NOTES

CHAPTER ONE:

1. Hugh & Glanville, *Formation and Function of Basic Body Tissues*, Appleton, 1971, p.2.
2. Orton & Neuhaus, *Biochemistry*, C.V. Mosby, 1970. pp. 12-13.
3. *Op cit*. Hugh & Glanville, p.3
4. *Ibid*. p.4

CHAPTER TWO:

1. Some authorities think there are ten essential amino acids, adding histidine and arginine to the list of eight, though some controversy exists as to the essentiality of histidine and arginine. How-

ever in injury and disease there is evidence that more amino acids than the so-called "essential eight" are needed to maintain the body nitrogen balance. (Abstract from Miller Laboratories, St. Louis, Mo., January, 1971).

2. Lappe, Frances M., *Diet for a Small Planet*, Ballantine, New York, 1971, Food protein continuum chart, p. 48.

3. Lappe's work, *Diet for a Small Planet*, is devoted to this study.

4. Orton & Neuhaus, *Biochemistry*, C.V. Mosby, 1970. pp. 330-331.

5. *Ibid*. pp. 331-333.

6. Halden, Dr. William, *The Framingham Study*, "Cholesterol in Food and Blood," 1970.

7. *Ibid*.

8. Fredericks, PhD., Carlton & Bailey, Herbert, *Foods, Facts, and Fallacies*. Arc Publications, 1969, p. 196.

9. Bellew, M.D. Bernard A. Los Angeles Times, 6-10-71.

10. Fredericks, PhD. Carlton, Proceedings from 13th Annual Symposium of the International College of Applied Nutrition, LaHabra, California. 1973.

11. Taber, C.W. & Assoc. *Cyclopedic Medical Dictionary*, 4th Edition, Davis Co., Philadelphia, 1946, p. 127.

12. Jones, M.D. & Hoerr, M.D., N.L., ed., *Medical Dictionary*, Blakiston, Philadelphia, 1951, "Protein" p. 823.

13. *Ibid*.

14.   H.A. & Blanck, F.C., *Nutritional Data*, Heinz Nutritional Research Division, Mellon Institute, Pittsburgh Pennsylvania, 1949. p 55.

15. Taber, & Assoc. *Op Cit.* p. 127.
16. *Ibid.*
17. Wooster & Blanck, *Op Cit.* p 55.
18. Neuhaus, Orton, *Op Cit.* pp 345-346.
19. "Brief", *Technical Data for the Physician*, Abstract from Enzyme Process Co., Van Nuys, California.
20. Food and Nutrition Board, National Research Council, 1968, p. 841.
21. U.S. Department of Agriculture, Handbook #8; H.J. Heinz Co., *Op Cit.*

CHAPTER THREE:

1. Taber, C.W. & Assoc., *Cyclopedic Medical Dictionary*, 4th Edition, Davis Co., Philadelphia, 1946, C-12.
2. Orton & Neuhaus, *Biochemistry*, C.V. Mosby, 1970. p. 166.
3. *Ibid.* 162-165.
4. *Ibid.* 159-161.
5. Taber, C.W. *Op. Cit.*, S-93.
6. Orton & Neuhaus, *Op. Cit.* 182-184.
7. *Ibid.* 171.
8. *Ibid.*
9. *Ibid.*
10. Taber, C.W. *Op Cit.* E-42.
11. Israel S., *Human Biochemistry,* 2nd Edition, C.V. Mosby. St. Louis. 1948., p. 364.
12. Orton & Neuhaus, *Op. Cit.* p. 192.
13. *Ibid.*
14. & Blanck, F.C., *Nutritional Data*, H.J. Heinz Co., Pittsburgh, 1949. p. 11.
15. *Ibid.* p. 12.
16. *Ibid.* p. 13.

17. Knudson, *Op. Cit.*, p. 374; Orton & Neuhaus, p. 204, 264.
18. Do not confuse Co-enzyme A with Vitamin A, a fat soluble co-enzyme, retinol, which is not at all involved, as far as we know, with carbohydrate metabolism.
19. *Ibid.* p. 373.
20. *Ibid.* p. 374.
21. cf. Stephenson, William K., *Concepts in Biochemistry,* Wiley & Sons, New York, 1967. p. 15, 21; Flood, W.E., *Dictionary of Chemical Names,* Littlefield-Adams, New Jersey, 1967, p. 25, 95.
22. Knudson, *Op. Cit.,* p. 374; Orton & Neuhaus, *Op. Cit.,* pp. 204, 264.
23. *Ibid.*
24. Orton & Neuhaus, *Op. Cit.*
25. Citric Acid to Isocitric, to succinic, to keto-glutaric, to malic, to fumaric, to pyruvic; this is known as the citric acid, or Krebs, cycle.
26. Knudson, *Op. Cit.* p. 374.
27. *Ibid.*
28. Orton & Neuhaus, *Op. Cit.* p. 204.
29. Knudson, Jr. M.D., Alfred G., "The Biochemical Role of B Vitamins in Metabolism," *Journal of Applied Nutrition,* Vol. 9, No. 12, 1956, p. 373.

CHAPTER FOUR:

1. Orton, James H. & Neuhaus, Otto W., *Biochemistry*, C.V. Mosby, 1971, p. 320.
2. Hanson, William A., *Physician's Diet Reference*, Enzyme Process Co., Van Nuys, California, 1961.
3. *Ibid.*
4. Taber, C.W. & Assoc., *Cyclopedic Medical Dic-*

tionary, 4th Edition, Davis Co., Philadelphia, 1946, F-78.

5. Hanson, *Op. Cit.* "Inositol".
   Orton & Neuhaus, *Op. Cit.* p. 832.

6. *Ibid.*, 304.

7. *Ibid.*

8. *Ibid.*

9. *Ibid.*, 302, which includes the statement, . . ."lipotropic, which simply means they prevent or cure fatty livers. . ."

10. *Ibid.* 303, 352-356.

11. *Ibid.* 303.

12. *Ibid.* 303, cf. Note #9.

13. Taber, C.W. *Op. Cit.* pp. B-23 — B-24.

14. *Ibid.*

15. *Ibid.* F 7-8.

16. *Ibid.*

17. *Ibid.*

18. *Ibid.*

19. Orton & Neuhaus, *Op. Cit*, p. 581, Table 19-3.

20. *Ibid.* pp. 293-297.

21. Knudson, Jr. Alfred G., "The Biochemical Role of B Vitamins in Metabolism," Journal of Applied Nutrition, Vol. 9, No. 2., 1956. pp. 373-374.

22. Orton & Neuhaus, *Op. Cit.* pp. 277, 788.

23. *Ibid.*

24. There have been many recent reliable works on Vitamin E, the most popular of which has been written by Dr. Wilfrid Schute, M.D., *Vitamin E, Your Key to a Healthy Heart*. This book offers the evidence of Dr. Schute's wide range of clinical experience with Vitamin E's remarkable healing qualities. According to Dr. Schute, in addition to its anti-oxidant functions, the vitamin

is chiefly instrumental in the prevention and cure of heart disease. Dr. Passwater's experiments with Vitamin E likewise show that it is involved with electron transfer which supports the implications made in current biochemistry textbooks (Orton & Neuhaus, 1971, p. 789).

CHAPTER FIVE:

1. Brubaker, Albert P., *Textbook of Human Physiology*, Blakiston & Co., Philadelphia, 1925, 8th edition, pp. 217-219.
2. *Ibid*. p. 214.
3. *Ibid*. p. 214.
4. *Applied Trophology*, Vol. 16, No. 1. "Constipation," Standard Process Laboratories, Milwaukee, Wisconsin, 1973. pp. 6-7.
5. *Ibid*.
6. *Ibid*. pp. 7-8.
7. *Ibid*. p. 6.
8. *Applied Trophology*, "The Diabetic Syndrome," Standard Process Laboratories, Milwaukee, March 1957. p. 4.

CHAPTER SIX:

1. Orton & Neuhaus, Biochemistry, C.V. Mosby, 1970. p. 800.
2. *Ibid*.
3. Hanson, Wm., *The Physician's Diet Reference*, Van Nuys, California. 1961.
4. Wooster, Jr. H.A., & Blanck, Fred C. *Nutritional Data*, H.J. Heinz, Pittsburgh, 1949. p. 23.
5. *Ibid*.
   Hanson, *Op. Cit.*
6. *Ibid*.

7. Taber, Clarence W., *Cyclopedic Medical Dictionary*, F.A. Davis Co., Philadelphia, 1946, S-54.
8. *Ibid.*
9. Hugh, A.E., & Glanville, J.N., *Formation and Function of Basic Body Tissues.* Appleton-Century-Crofts, 1971. pp. 18-22.
10. Orton & Neuhaus, *Op. Cit.* p. 768.
11. *Ibid.*
12. *Ibid.*
13. *Ibid.* 772.
14. cf. The Analysis of Levels of Vitamin A Toxicity Report in the FDA Bibliography in which toxic doses for adults were in the range of 90,000-600,000 U.S.P. daily for a period of three months onward. With young children, toxicity varied determined by the age and the amount given.
15. Kirschmann, John D., *Nutrition Almanac*, Nutrition, Bismarck, N. Dakota, 1972. p. 52.
16. Hanson, *Op. Cit.* "Vitamin K."
17. Orten and Neuhaus, *Op. Cit.* pp. 619-622.
18. *Ibid.*
19. Orten & Neuhaus, *Op. Cit.*, p. 790.
20. *Ibid.* p. 778.
21. Flood, W.E., *Dictionary of Chemical Names*, Littlefield Adams, New Jersey, 1967. pp. 55, 65, 89, Pfeiffer, Dr. E.E., *Balanced Nutrition*, unpublished manuscript, 1958. p. 16.
22. Orten & Neuhaus, *Op. Cit.* pp. 779-780.
23. *Ibid.* pp. 784-785.
24. Taber, *Op. Cit.* pp. B-45.
25. Kirschmann, John D., *Nutrition Almanac*, Bismarck, North Dakota, 1972, p. 48.
26. Orten & Neuhaus, *Op. Cit.* pp. 272 ff.
27. Pfeiffer, Dr. E.E., *Op. Cit.* p. 8, 10.

28. Orten & Neuhaus, *Op. Cit.* pp. 213-214; 299-300.
29. Pfeiffer, *Op. Cit.* p. 11.
30. Hanson, *Op. Cit.* "Vitamin E."
31. Berst, Marvin, "Vitamin E— The Better Treatment for Burns." *Prevention* Magazine, January 1973, pp. 98-103.
32. Davidson, *Biochemistry of Nucleic Acids*, Methuen Monographs, 1960, cited by Hanson, Wm. A.,in *Brief, Technical Data for the Physician*, Enzyme Process Laboratories, Van Nuys, 1968.
33. Orten & Neuhaus, *Op. Cit.* p. 105. Fig. 6-8.
34. Wooster & Blanck, *Op. Cit.* p. 12.
                    "B2 (Riboflavin)" in *Physicians Diet Reference*.
35. Wooster & Blanck, *Op. Cit.* p. 12.
    Hanson, Wm. A.,*Op. Cit.* "B2 (Riboflavin)..
36. Hanson, *Ibid.* "B12" and "Folic Acid".
37. "Folic Acid," Towne Paulsen, Pharmaceutical Chemists, Monrovia, California.
38. *Ibid.*
39. Hanson. *Op. Cit.* "Folic Acid."
40. *Ibid.* "Folic Acid — Associated Physiology."
41. *Ibid.* "B-12: Basic Action and Associated Physiology."
42. *Ibid.* "Biotin: Basic Action and Associated Factors."
43. Wooster & Blanck. p. 21. Bilineurine performs this positive function as acetylcholine.

CHAPTER SEVEN:

1. Taber, Clarence W., *Cyclopedic Medical Dictionary*, 4th Edition, F.A. Davis. Co., Philadelphia, 2946, p. B-45.
2. Orten & Neuhaus, *Biochemistry*, C.V. Mosby, St.

Louis, 1970. p. 549.

3. *Ibid*. p. 594.

4. Taber, *Op. Cit*. p. P-54.

5. *Ibid*. p. P-64.

6. Orten & Neuhaus, *Op. Cit*. p. 436.

7. *Ibid*. p. 436.

8. *Ibid*. pp. 620-626.

9. Grant, J.C. Boileau, *An Atlas of Anatomy*. 5th Edition, Williams & Wilkins Co., Baltimore, 1962. Fig. 415, 416, 422.

10. Hugh, A.E., *The Cardiovascular System*, Appleton-Century-Crofts, 1971. pp. 19-21.

11. Fredericks, PhD., Carlton, *Proceedings from 13th Annual Symposium of ICAN*, La Habra, California, 1973.

12. *Ibid*. Hugh, p. 21.

13. Grant, *Op. Cit*. Fig. 421.

14. Hugh, *Op. Cit*. pp. 7-12; Grant, *Op. Cit*. Fig. 435.

15. Snively, M.D., William D., & Thurbach, Jan., *Sea of Life*, David McKay Co., New York, 1969. p. 24.

16. Hugh, A.E., *Op. Cit*. pp. 11-12. Pfeiffer, M.D., E.E., *Balanced Nutrition*, unpublished manuscript. 1958. Min.-7.

17. Orten & Neuhaus, *Op. Cit*. p. 413.

18. Bowman's capsule. cf. Brubaker, Albert P., *Textbook of Physiology*, 8th Edition, Blakiston, Philadelphia, 1925, p. 501.

19. Orten & Neuhaus, *Op. Cit*. p. 718.

20. *Ibid*.

21. *Ibid*. 720.

22. Miller,PhD. John J., "Chelation: A New Approach to the Practice of Medicine. *"Journal of Applied Nutrition."* Vol. 15. No. 3 & 4, p. 193.

23. *Ibid*. 193.

210

24. *Ibid*. pp. 192-202.
25. *Ibid*. p. 201.
26. *Ibid*. p. 197.
27. *Ibid*.
28. Snively, *Op. Cit* pp. 18-19.
29. *Ibid*.
30. *Ibid*. p. 17.

BIBLIOGRAPHY

1. "Applied Trophology." Vol. 1. No. 3. Standard Process Laboratories, Milwaukee, 1957.
2. "Applied Trophology," Vol. 16. No. 1. Standard Process Laboratories, Milwaukee, Wisconsin, 1973.
3. *An Atlas of Anatomy*, J.C. Boileau, 5th Edition. Williams & Wilkins Co., Baltimore, 1962.
4. *Balanced Nutrition*, Dr. E.E. Pfeiffer, M.D. unpublished manuscript, 1958.
5. *Biochemistry*, James H. Orten & Otto W. Neuhaus, C.V. Mosby. Saint Louis, 1970.
6. "Bulletin," Miller Laboratories, St. Louis, January, 1971.
7. *The Cardiovasular System*, A.E. Hugh, Appleton-Century-Crofts, 1971.
8. *Composition and Facts About Food*, Ford Heritage, Health Research, Molekumne Hill, California, 1968.
9. *Composition of Foods*, Agriculture Handbook #8, U.S. Department of Agriculture, Revised December, 1963.
10. *Concepts in Biochemistry*, William K. Stephenson, Wiley & Sons, New York, 1967.
11. *Cyclopedic Medical Dictionary*, 4th Edition, Taber, C.W. & Associates, Davis Co., Phila-

delphia, 1946.

12. *Diet for a Small Planet*, Frances M. Lappe, Ballantine, New York, 1971.

13. *Formation and Function of Basic Body Tissues*, A.E. Hugh & J.N. Glanville, Appleton Century Crofts, New York and London, 1971.

14. *The Framingham Study*. Dr. William Halden, 1970.

15. *Human Biochemistry*, 2nd Edition, Israel S. Kleiner, C.V. Mosby, St. Louis, 1948.

16. "Journal of Applied Nutrition," Vol. 9, No. 2, 1956. International College of Applied Nutrition, La Habra, California.

17. *Medical Dictionary*, ed. Jones, M.D., H.W. & Hoerr, M.D., N.L., Blakiston, Philadelphia, 1951.

18. *Nutritional Data*, Wooster, Jr., H.A., & Blanck, F.C., Heinz Nutritional Research Division, Mellon Institute, Pittsburgh, Pennsylvania, 1949.

19. *Nutrition Almanac* Ed. John D. Kirschmann. Publ. "Nutrition", Bismarck, N. Dakota, 1972.

20. *The Physician's Diet Reference*, William A. Hanson, Van Nuys, California, 1961.

21. Proceedings from the 13th Annual Symposium of the International College of Applied Nutrition, La Habra, California, 1973.

22. *Sea of Life*, William D. Snively, M.D., and Jan Thurbach, David McKay Co., New York, 1969.

23. *Technical Data for the Physician*, abstracts from Enzyme Process Co., Van Nuys, California. Wm. A. Hanson, Editor.

24. *A Textbook of Human Physiology*, Albert P. Brubaker, Blakiston & Son Co., Philadelphia, 8th Edition, 1925.

212